SINGLE
Serves
cook solo with style

MURDOCH BOOKS

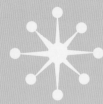

Cooking for one means you only have to please yourself. And in this book you'll find tantalising ways to do just that — with speed and simplicity, and no need to halve or cut down on quantities. There are dishes to suit all tastes, from Thai fish cakes to spiced chicken quesadillas, from a slow-cooked mini lamb roast to a crisp-skin blue eye trevalla fillet that cooks in minutes. And because it's sometimes good to come home to an already cooked meal, many recipes make two serves and include tips for storing and transforming the second serve into a different dish for another day. Living solo shouldn't mean missing out on the pleasure of cooking and eating tasty, balanced meals. Make the most of it.

Contents

06 *Light meals*

Fresh ideas for delicious light meals and substantial snacks for one. A soufflé omelette with ham and gruyère cheese could be just the thing at the end of a long day, a sesame beef salad with avocado makes a perfect lunch on the run and tasty tuna empanadas hit the spot any time.

76 *Mains*

Simple and innovative main meals for one person that don't compromise on flavour or quality. Try poached beef with horseradish cream, chargrilled piri-piri spatchcock, whole fish steamed with Chinese flavours or lamb steak with pecorino mash and artichokes.

146 *Desserts*

Cooking for one? That means you don't have to share dessert! Go ahead and spoil yourself with peanut brittle ice cream with chocolate sauce, or maybe you'd prefer a luscious cherry-brioche trifle, a brandy-caramel pear or grilled figs topped with honeyed mascarpone …

Light meals

Orecchiette with chicken sausage, tomato, rocket and parmesan • Spiced lamb and yoghurt in pitta bread • Thai fish cakes with tomato salad • Fennel, tomato and fish soup with aïoli • Tuna empanadas • Golden haloumi with bean and olive salad • Soft cheese and walnut polenta with mushrooms • Sesame beef salad with avocado and grapefruit • Chicken, corn and noodle soup • Pumpkin and prosciutto pizza with hazelnut salad • Chargrilled squid and pasta salad • Warm eggplant and feta salad • Soufflé omelette with ham and gruyère cheese • Tortellini stracciatella • Pork, brie and apricot sandwich • Thai-style steamed mussels • Spiced chicken quesadillas • Beef and cashew noodle salad • Garlicky white bean brandade • Prawn and bok choy omelette • Spicy capsicum and tomato bake with egg • Lamb, barley and mint salad • Ravioli with zucchini, sage and pine nuts • Individual fondue • Smoked salmon and chargrilled vegetable panzanella • Lamb burger with hummus and beetroot • Roast asparagus and tofu salad with sesame dressing • Smoked chicken Waldorf salad on bruschetta • Tuna Niçoise salad • BBQ duck and hoisin wrap • Caramel tofu with peanuts and ginger • Pastrami and fontina croque monsieur • Lamb, lemon and rice soup • Smoked fish rarebit

Preparation time: 10 minutes   **Cooking time:** 20 minutes   **Serves:** 1

Orecchiette with chicken sausage, tomato, rocket and parmesan

90 g (3¼ oz/¾ cup) orecchiette pasta
1 tablespoon extra virgin olive oil
150 g (5½ oz) chicken sausages
  (about 2 small), skins removed
1 garlic clove, crushed
2 anchovy fillets, chopped
pinch chilli flakes (optional)
2½ tablespoons white wine
125 g (4½ oz/¾ cup) cherry
  tomatoes, halved
1 tablespoon cream
1 small handful rocket (arugula)
shaved parmesan, to serve

Bring a large saucepan of salted water to the boil. Add the orecchiette and cook according to packet instructions or until al dente. Drain and set aside.

Place the oil in a heavy-based frying pan over medium–high heat. Add the sausage meat and cook for 1–2 minutes, stirring to break the meat up. Reduce the heat to low, add the garlic, anchovies and chilli, if using, and cook, stirring, for 1 minute or until the anchovies have melted. Pour in the wine and cook until it has reduced by half. Add the tomatoes and cook for 5 minutes or until collapsing. Add the cream and rocket and cook for another minute or until the cream is heated through and the rocket is wilted. Season to taste with sea salt and freshly ground black pepper.

Add the cooked orecchiette to the sauce and toss to combine well. Spoon into a serving bowl, top with the parmesan and serve immediately.

Spiced lamb and yoghurt in pitta bread

½ teaspoon ground cumin
½ teaspoon sweet paprika
¼ teaspoon dried oregano
2 tablespoons olive oil
2 tablespoons lemon juice
200 g (7 oz) lamb back strap
  (or 3 lamb fillets)
125 g (4½ oz) tin chickpeas (garbanzo
  beans), rinsed and drained
1 small garlic clove, crushed
2 tablespoons Greek-style yoghurt
1 tablespoon finely chopped mint
½ teaspoon caster (superfine) sugar
1 pitta bread, warmed through
2 baby cos (romaine) lettuce
  leaves, shredded
1 roma (plum) tomato, sliced

Combine the cumin, paprika, oregano, 1 tablespoon of the olive oil and 1 tablespoon of the lemon juice in a small shallow bowl. Add the mixture to the lamb, rubbing to coat it, then cover and let stand for 5–10 minutes.

Meanwhile, combine the chickpeas with the garlic and the remaining oil and lemon juice, and 2 tablespoons of warm water in a food processor and process until a coarse purée forms.

Place the yoghurt, mint and sugar in a small bowl, mix well to combine, then set aside.

Heat a chargrill or frying pan over high heat. Add the lamb and cook for 2–3 minutes each side. Place on a plate and loosely cover with foil for 3 minutes.

Top the pitta bread with the chickpea purée, shredded lettuce, tomato and sliced lamb. Drizzle with the minted yoghurt and serve immediately, with extra minted yoghurt on the side.

✳ **Preparation time:** 15 minutes　　✳ **Cooking time:** 5 minutes　　✳ **Serves:** 1

Preparation time: 20 minutes, plus 30 minutes chilling

Cooking time: 5 minutes

Serves: 1

Thai fish cakes with tomato salad

150 g (5½ oz) red fish or flathead fillets,
  skin removed
1 small egg yolk
1 teaspoon Thai red curry paste
1 teaspoon sweet chilli sauce
1 teaspoon fish sauce
1 small kaffir lime leaf, finely shredded
2 green beans, very thinly sliced
1 tablespoon chopped coriander
  (cilantro) leaves
1 tablespoon peanut oil
steamed jasmine rice and lime wedges,
  to serve

Tomato salad
1 small handful coriander (cilantro) leaves
1 small handful mint
½ Lebanese (short) cucumber,
  halved lengthways, seeds removed
  and sliced on the diagonal
¼ avocado, chopped
5 cherry tomatoes, halved
1 tablespoon crushed unsalted
  roasted peanuts

Chilli dressing
2 teaspoons lime juice
2 teaspoons fish sauce
2 teaspoons sweet chilli sauce

Place the fish into a small food processor and process until smooth, or finely chop with a very sharp knife. Transfer to a bowl and add the egg yolk, curry paste, sweet chilli sauce, fish sauce, lime leaf, beans and coriander. Mix until well combined, then roll heaped tablespoons of the mixture into balls and flatten each into a disc about 5 cm (2 inches) across. Cover and refrigerate for 30 minutes.

To make the tomato salad, combine all the ingredients except the peanuts in a bowl. Sprinkle with the peanuts.

To make the chilli dressing, combine all the ingredients in a bowl and whisk until well combined.

Heat the oil in a small non-stick frying pan over medium heat. Cook the fish cakes for 2–3 minutes on each side or until golden and firm to the touch.

To serve, arrange the fish cakes on a plate. Top with the salad and spoon over the dressing. Serve with steamed rice and lime wedges.

Fennel, tomato and fish soup with aïoli

2 teaspoons olive oil
2 spring onions (scallions), white part
  only, thinly sliced
½ fennel bulb, trimmed and thinly
  sliced lengthways
1 garlic clove, crushed
¼ teaspoon fennel seeds
pinch dried chilli flakes (optional)
1 tablespoon finely diced carrot
1 tablespoon finely diced celery
1 small vine-ripened tomato,
  finely chopped
60 ml (2 fl oz/¼ cup) dry white wine
500 ml (17 fl oz/2 cups) fish or
  chicken stock
¼ teaspoon saffron threads (optional)
150 g (5½ oz) firm white fish, skin and
  bones removed and cut into 4 cm
  (1½ inch) pieces
3 mussels, bearded and scrubbed
2 teaspoons aïoli
2 teaspoons chopped flat-leaf
  (Italian) parsley
crusty bread, to serve

Heat the oil in a small saucepan over a medium–
low heat. Add the spring onion and fennel, and
cook, stirring for 5–7 minutes or until tender.
Add the garlic, fennel seeds and chilli, if using,
and cook, stirring, for 1 minute.

Stir in the carrot, celery, tomato, white wine,
stock and saffron, if using. Increase the heat to
medium–high, bring to the boil, then reduce the
heat and cook gently for 5 minutes.

Add the fish and mussels, cover and cook
gently for 2 minutes or until the fish is tender
and the mussels open. (Discard any unopened
mussels.) Season to taste with sea salt and
freshly ground black pepper. Spoon into a bowl,
top with aïoli and scatter with parsley. Serve
immediately with bread on the side.

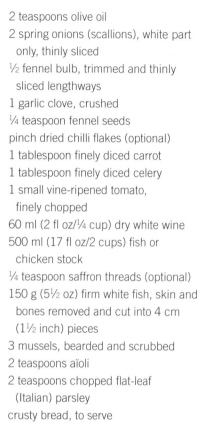

Preparation time: 10 minutes   Cooking time: 15 minutes   Serves: 1

❋ Preparation time: 20 minutes   **❋ Cooking time:** 45 minutes   **❋ Serves:** 1

Tuna empanadas

flour, for dusting
2 tablespoons olive oil
1 small onion, finely chopped
1 garlic clove, finely chopped
½ small red capsicum (pepper),
  seeded and cut into 1.5 cm
  (⅝ inch) pieces
1 teaspoon cumin seeds
½ teaspoon smoked paprika
1 teaspoon dried oregano
1 roma (plum) tomato, seeded and cut
  into 1.5 cm (⅝ inch) pieces
2 tablespoons pitted green
  olives, chopped
2 tablespoons raisins, chopped
185 g (6½ oz) tin tuna in oil, drained
2 tablespoons chopped parsley
2 sheets frozen shortcrust
  pastry, thawed
1 egg, lightly beaten

Preheat the oven to 200°C (400°F/Gas 6). Lightly dust a baking tray with flour.

Heat the oil in a frying pan over medium heat. Cook the onion for 5 minutes, or until softened. Add the garlic and capsicum and cook for 5 minutes. Stir in the cumin, paprika, oregano, tomato, olives and raisins. Cook for another 5 minutes, or until softened slightly. Remove from the heat, then cool to room temperature.

Flake the tuna with a fork in a bowl, then add the tomato mixture and parsley and season to taste with sea salt. Stir to combine well.

Cut four 14 cm (5½ inch) circles from the pastry. Spoon filling onto one side of each circle. Dampen the pastry edges with water. Fold the pastry over the filling, to form a pastie shape. Seal the edges with the tines of a fork. Brush with the egg and make a slit on the top using the tip of a knife. Transfer to the floured baking tray. Bake in the preheated oven for 25–30 minutes or until the pastry is golden brown.

This recipe makes 4 empanadas. They are suitable for freezing either before or after baking. Thaw in the refrigerator when ready to cook. If using raw-dough empanadas, cook thawed pastries as described in the method. If reheating baked empanadas, heat in a 140°C (275°F/Gas 1) oven for 12–15 minutes.

Golden haloumi with bean and olive salad

30 g (1 oz) green beans, ends trimmed
  (about 12)
1 tablespoon small black olives
2 sun-dried tomatoes in oil, drained
  and chopped
baby oregano leaves, to serve
1 tablespoon olive oil
125 g (4½ oz) haloumi cheese, cut into
  three slices about 8 mm (⅜ inch) thick
lemon cheeks, to serve (optional)

Lemon and honey dressing
2 tablespoons extra virgin olive oil
1 tablespoon lemon juice
1 tablespoon honey, warmed
1 teaspoon fresh oregano,
  roughly chopped

To make the lemon and honey dressing, place all the ingredients in a small bowl and whisk to combine well, then season to taste with sea salt and freshly ground black pepper and set aside.

Cook the beans in a small saucepan of boiling salted water for 2 minutes or until just tender. Drain and transfer the beans to a bowl of iced water to stop the cooking process. When the beans have cooled, drain well.

Place the beans, olives and tomatoes in a bowl. Pour over a tablespoon of the dressing and toss to coat evenly. Pile the salad onto a serving plate and scatter with oregano leaves.

Heat the oil in a small frying pan over medium heat, add the haloumi slices and cook for 1 minute on each side or until golden. Arrange the haloumi alongside the prepared salad. Serve immediately with the dressing and lemon cheeks, if using, on the side.

✳ **Preparation time:** 20 minutes ✳ **Cooking time:** 5 minutes ✳ **Serves:** 1

Preparation time: 10 minutes   **Cooking time:** 15 minutes   **Serves:** 1

Soft cheese and walnut polenta with mushrooms

2 large field mushrooms, trimmed
 and peeled
1 tablespoon olive oil
310 ml (10¾ fl oz/1¼ cups)
 chicken stock
60 ml (2 fl oz/¼ cup) milk
45 g (1¾ oz/¼ cup) instant polenta
15 g (½ oz) butter
30 g (1 oz/¼ cup) walnut pieces, toasted
 and chopped
2 tablespoons shaved pecorino cheese
chopped chives, to serve

Heat a chargrill pan or small, heavy-based frying pan over medium heat. Brush the mushrooms with the oil and cook, cap side down, for 3 minutes, then turn and cook for 3–4 minutes or until the mushrooms are tender. Remove from the heat, cover and set aside.

Combine the chicken stock and milk in a small saucepan and bring to the boil over medium heat. Stirring constantly, gradually add the polenta in a steady stream, then cook, whisking constantly, until the mixture boils and thickens. Reduce the heat to low and cook, stirring often, for 5–6 minutes or until the mixture is very thick. Remove from the heat and add the butter and most of the walnuts and pecorino, reserving some for garnish. Mix well to combine.

To serve, spoon the polenta into a shallow bowl, top with the mushrooms, garnish with the remaining walnuts and pecorino, sprinkle with the chives and serve immediately.

Instead of pecorino, you can use a good-quality parmesan cheese.

Sesame beef salad with avocado and grapefruit

To make ginger juice, place peeled and chopped fresh ginger in a garlic crusher and crush lightly to extract the juice. If short on time use slices of rare roast beef from your supermarket or deli.

1 small ruby grapefruit
150 g (5½ oz) beef eye fillet
1 teaspoon olive oil
1 large handful watercress sprigs or
  rocket (arugula)
½ avocado, sliced
1 tablespoon chopped chives

Ginger dressing
2 teaspoons olive oil
2 teaspoons sherry
1 teaspoon white wine vinegar
¼ teaspoon sesame oil
¼ teaspoon fresh ginger juice (*see tip*)
2 teaspoons toasted sesame seeds

To make the ginger dressing, place all the ingredients in a small bowl and whisk until well combined.

Using a small sharp knife, peel the grapefruit, taking care to remove all the white pith. Then carefully remove the segments by cutting between the white membrane and flesh. Set aside.

Heat a small, heavy-based frying pan or chargrill pan over high heat. Brush the beef with oil, then cook for 1 minute on each side for rare, or until cooked to your liking. Remove the steak to a plate and cool to room temperature.

Place the watercress sprigs on a serving plate. Slice the beef thinly across the grain and arrange on the watercress. Top with the sliced avocado and grapefruit. Sprinkle with the chives. Drizzle the salad with the dressing and serve immediately.

☀ **Preparation time:** 12 minutes   ☀ **Cooking time:** 5 minutes   ☀ **Serves:** 1

Preparation time: 15 minutes, plus 30 minutes standing ✳ **Cooking time:** 10 minutes ✳ **Serves:** 1 + 1

Chicken, corn and noodle soup

5 g (⅛ oz/¼ cup) sliced
  shiitake mushrooms
3 teaspoons vegetable or peanut oil
1½ teaspoons finely chopped ginger
1 spring onion (scallion), trimmed
  and finely chopped
1 corn cob, trimmed and kernels
  removed (about 1 cup of kernels)
310 ml (10¾ fl oz/1¼ cups)
  chicken stock
1 chicken breast fillet, thinly sliced
1 tablespoon soy sauce, plus extra,
  to serve
1 tablespoon Chinese rice wine
  or dry sherry
1 baby bok choy (pak choy), trimmed
  and thinly sliced
1 x 62 g (2¼ oz) 'cake' dried egg noodles
  (sold in Asian section of supermarkets)
sesame oil, coriander (cilantro) sprigs
  and toasted sesame seeds, to serve

Place the shiitake mushrooms in a small bowl and pour over 125 ml (4 fl oz/½ cup) boiling water. Stand for 30 minutes or until the mushrooms are softened, then drain well, reserving the liquid. Remove the stems and slice the mushrooms thinly.

Heat the oil in a heavy-based saucepan over medium heat. Add the ginger and spring onion and cook, stirring, for 30 seconds, then add the mushrooms and corn and cook for 1 minute. Increase the heat to high, add the stock, 310 ml (10¾ fl oz/1¼ cups) water and the reserved mushroom liquid and bring to the boil. Simmer for 2–3 minutes, then reduce the heat to low, add the chicken, soy sauce, rice wine and bok choy and cook for 1 minute or until the chicken is just cooked through and the bok choy is wilted.

Meanwhile, place the noodles in a small saucepan, cover with boiling water, then boil over high heat for 2 minutes. Drain well. Place the noodles in a warmed bowl, then ladle over the soup. Add a few drops of sesame oil, to taste, then garnish with a few coriander sprigs and sesame seeds and serve immediately.

This recipe makes enough soup for two serves. Simply freeze left-over soup in an airtight container until required. Just before serving, cook one 62 g (2¼ oz) 'cake' of dried egg noodles and serve as described in the method.

Pumpkin and prosciutto pizza with hazelnut salad

1 tablespoon olive oil, plus extra,
  for greasing
1 garlic clove, crushed
150 g (5½ oz/1 cup) butternut pumpkin,
  (squash) peeled, seeded and cut into
  1 cm (½ inch) pieces
60 ml (2 fl oz/¼ cup) tomato pasta sauce
50 g (1¾ oz) prosciutto (about 4 thin
  slices), torn
100 g (3½ oz) taleggio or mozzarella
  cheese, cut into 5 mm (¼ inch) slices
1 small handful mixed salad leaves
1 small handful basil
1 tablespoon hazelnuts, roasted, peeled
  and coarsely chopped
1 teaspoon extra virgin olive oil

Pizza dough
large pinch caster (superfine) sugar
2 teaspoons active dry yeast
300 g (10½ oz/2 cups) plain (all-purpose)
  flour, plus extra for kneading
½ teaspoon salt
2 tablespoons extra virgin olive oil

To make the pizza dough, combine 200 ml (7 fl oz) warm water and the sugar in a small bowl, sprinkle over the yeast, then stand in a warm, draught-free place for 7 minutes or until foamy. Combine the flour and salt in a bowl. Add the yeast mixture and oil, then mix until a coarse dough forms. Turn out onto a lightly floured surface and knead for 5 minutes, or until smooth and elastic, adding a little extra flour, if necessary, if dough remains sticky. Lightly oil a bowl, add the dough and turn to coat with oil, then cover the bowl and stand in a draught-free place for 1 hour, or until the dough has doubled in size.

Preheat the oven to 220°C (425°F/Gas 7). Combine the olive oil, garlic and pumpkin in a roasting pan and bake for 25 minutes or until the pumpkin is cooked through and browned lightly. Remove from the pan and set aside.

Knock the dough back, then divide into four even pieces. Using a rolling pin, roll each piece of dough out to a round about 18 cm (7 inches) across. Wrap three in plastic wrap, place in an airtight, ziplock bag and freeze for up to 3 weeks, for later use. Place the remaining dough base on a lightly greased baking tray.

Spread the pasta sauce over the pizza base, then arrange the prosciutto, pumpkin and cheese slices over, leaving a 1 cm (½ inch) border around the edge of the dough. Bake for 12 minutes or until the cheese has melted and the pizza is golden brown.

Meanwhile, place the salad leaves and basil in a small bowl, add the nuts and oil, then season to taste with sea salt and freshly ground black pepper. Top the hot pizza with the salad and serve immediately.

Preparation time: 20 minutes, plus 1 hour 10 minutes standing   **Cooking time:** 40 minutes   **Serves:** 1 + 1

✳ Preparation time: 15 minutes   **✳ Cooking time:** 15 minutes   **✳ Serves:** 1

Chargrilled squid and pasta salad

80 g (2¾ oz) linguine pasta
1 tomato, trimmed and finely diced
¼ head radicchio
   (about ¾ cup), shredded
8 flat-leaf (Italian) parsley leaves
8 basil leaves
2 tablespoons Ligurian or other small
   black olives
2 anchovy fillets, finely chopped
1 small garlic clove, crushed
2 teaspoons lemon juice
2 tablespoons olive oil
120 g (4¼ oz) cleaned squid tubes and
   tentacles, tubes cut open and inside
   surface scored finely with a small,
   sharp knife
lemon wedges, to serve

Cook the linguine in a saucepan of boiling, salted water for 12 minutes or according to the packet instructions until al dente. Drain, then cool under cold water and drain again.

Combine the tomato, radicchio, parsley, basil and olives in a bowl, then add the linguine and toss to combine. Lightly whisk together the anchovy, garlic, lemon juice and olive oil. Drizzle over the pasta salad.

Heat a chargrill pan over high heat or a barbecue to high. Cook the squid tubes and tentacles for 3 minutes, turning once, or until lightly charred and cooked through. Add to the salad, toss well to combine and serve immediately with lemon wedges.

Warm eggplant and feta salad

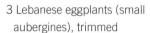

3 Lebanese eggplants (small
  aubergines), trimmed
1 tablespoon olive oil
1 small handful mint
35 g (1¼ oz/¼ cup) crumbled firm
  feta cheese
6 semi-dried tomatoes

Yoghurt dressing
1½ tablespoons Greek-style yoghurt
¼ teaspoon ground cumin
½ garlic clove, crushed

To make the yoghurt dressing, combine the
yoghurt, cumin, garlic and 1 teaspoon water
in a small bowl and stir to combine well.
Season to taste with sea salt and freshly ground
black pepper. Set aside.

Cut the eggplants in half lengthways. Heat
the oil in a heavy-based frying pan over medium
heat and cook the eggplant, cut side down,
for 2 minutes, then turn and cook for another
2 minutes or until cooked through. Place on
a serving plate, scatter over the mint, feta
and tomatoes, drizzle with the yoghurt dressing
and serve immediately.

Preparation time: 5 minutes   **Cooking time:** 5 minutes   **Serves:** 1

Soufflé omelette with ham and gruyère cheese

50 g (1¾ oz) smoked ham
  (about 1 thin slice), chopped
1 teaspoon dijon mustard
2 eggs, separated
1 tablespoon cream
½ tablespoon butter
35 g (1¼ oz/¼ cup) grated
  gruyère cheese

Tomato salad

1 small roma (plum) tomato, chopped
2 semi-dried tomatoes, chopped
1 tablespoon finely chopped flat-leaf
  (Italian) parsley
pinch caster (superfine) sugar
1 tablespoon extra virgin olive oil

Combine the ham and mustard in a small bowl, then mix to coat the ham. Set aside.

Place the egg yolks and cream in a small bowl, whisk until combined, then season to taste with sea salt and freshly ground black pepper. Place the egg whites in a clean bowl and whisk until soft peaks form. Fold the egg whites into the yolk mixture.

Place a small non-stick frying pan over medium–low heat, add the butter, then heat until foaming. Add the egg mixture, spreading it to evenly cover the pan, then cook for 2 minutes or until the edges are set. Scatter the ham over, then sprinkle with the cheese. Cook for 2 minutes or until the omelette is puffy and the cheese is starting to melt. Fold the omelette over using a spatula and cook for 2 minutes more. Remove from the heat, then stand for 2 minutes.

To make the tomato salad, combine all the ingredients in a small bowl and toss until well combined.

Place the omelette on a serving plate, top with the salad and serve immediately.

Tortellini stracciatella

1 egg
1 tablespoon finely grated parmesan,
  plus extra, to serve
1 small handful rocket (arugula),
  coarsely chopped
310 ml (10¾ fl oz/1¼ cups)
  chicken stock
60 g (2¼ oz/¾ cup) frozen
  cheese-filled tortellini
35 g (1¼ oz/¼ cup) frozen baby peas

Beat the egg in a small bowl with a fork. Stir in the parmesan and rocket, then set aside.

Combine the chicken stock and 310 ml (10¾ fl oz/1¼ cups) water in a small saucepan, then bring to the boil. Add the tortellini and peas and simmer for 6–8 minutes or until tender. Remove the pan from the heat, then transfer the tortellini and peas with a slotted spoon to a warmed serving bowl. Spoon a few tablespoons of the hot cooking liquid over the pasta to keep moist.

Working quickly, pour the egg mixture into the cooking liquid in a thin stream, stirring lightly with a fork so the egg cooks in thin strands. Ladle the mixture over the pasta and peas and scatter with the extra parmesan. Season to taste with sea salt and freshly ground black pepper and serve immediately.

Preparation time: 15 minutes **Cooking time:** 10 minutes **Serves:** 1

Pork, brie and apricot sandwich

10 cm (4 inch) slice Turkish bread, cut in
half horizontally
3 teaspoons olive oil
1 small red onion, halved and
thinly sliced
½ baby fennel bulb, trimmed and
thinly sliced
1 x 120 g (4¼ oz) pork steak
1 tablespoon dijonnaise or other
purchased mustard mayonnaise
1 small handful baby spinach leaves
50 g (1¾ oz) brie cheese, sliced
4 tinned apricot halves, drained
(or use two ripe fresh apricots,
halved and stoned)

Toast the Turkish bread halves on both sides,
then set aside. Heat half the oil in a small frying
pan over medium heat, add the onion and fennel
and cook, stirring, for 5 minutes or until soft but
not browned. Transfer to a plate.

Pat the pork steak dry with paper towels.
Reheat the frying pan, add the remaining oil and
cook the pork steak for 2–3 minutes each side,
turning once, until cooked through. Set aside
for a few minutes, then cut into 3 or 4 slices
on the diagonal.

Place the toasted Turkish bread slices, crust
side down, on a large serving plate. Spread with
the dijonnaise, then arrange over the spinach
leaves, followed by the pork slices and fennel
mixture. Top each slice of bread with a slice of
brie and 2 apricot halves, securing these with
toothpicks, and serve immediately.

Leave out the fennel if unavailable.
You can replace Turkish bread with
ciabatta bread, if you like, and use
chutney instead of the dijonnaise.
Store left-over apricots in their juice
covered in a small bowl and eat with
cereal for breakfast.

Thai-style steamed mussels

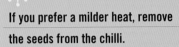

If you prefer a milder heat, remove the seeds from the chilli.

1 tablespoon vegetable oil
½ red bird's eye chilli, or to taste,
  thinly sliced
2 teaspoons finely grated fresh ginger
1 garlic clove, finely chopped
12 large black mussels, bearded
  and scrubbed
60 ml (2 fl oz/¼ cup) Chinese rice
  wine, or sweet sherry
1 small tomato, chopped
2 teaspoons fish sauce, or to taste
1 teaspoon lime juice
2½ teaspoons sugar, or to taste
1 small handful Thai basil or coriander
  (cilantro) leaves, plus extra, to serve
cooked fresh or dried rice vermicelli
  noodles, to serve
lime cheek, to serve

Place the oil in a saucepan with a tight-fitting lid over medium heat. When hot, add the chilli, ginger and garlic and cook, stirring, for 30–60 seconds or until fragrant, taking care not to burn the garlic. Add the mussels, rice wine and tomato, and shake the pan to combine well. Cover, then cook for 2–4 minutes, shaking the pan occasionally, or until the mussels open. (Discard any mussels that don't open.)

Remove from the heat and add the fish sauce, lime juice, sugar and Thai basil, tossing until basil begins to wilt. Top the rice noodles with the mussels and serve immediately with a lime cheek and extra basil.

☀ **Preparation time:** 15 minutes   ☀ **Cooking time:** 5 minutes   ☀ **Serves:** 1

❋ **Preparation time:** 10 minutes,
plus 1 hour chilling

❋ **Cooking time:** 15 minutes

❋ **Serves:** 1 + 1

Spiced chicken quesadillas

2½ tablespoons extra virgin olive oil
½ teaspoon dried oregano
½ teaspoon ground cumin
2 tablespoons lime juice
1 chicken breast fillet
4 soft flour tortillas
60 g (2¼ oz/½ cup) grated
  cheddar cheese
60 g (2¼ oz/¼ cup) grilled red capsicum
  (pepper), cut into thin strips (available
  from the supermarket deli counter)
2 tablespoons pickled sliced jalapeños,
  chopped (available from the
  supermarket)
2 tablespoons chopped coriander
  (cilantro) leaves
2 tablespoons tomato salsa
2 tablespoons sour cream

Combine 2 tablespoons of the olive oil with the oregano, cumin and lime juice in a bowl and whisk to combine well. Slice the chicken breast into 5 mm (¼ inch) wide strips, then add to the mixture in the bowl and toss to coat. Cover the bowl with plastic wrap and refrigerate for 1 hour or until needed. Drain the chicken. Place a non-stick frying pan over medium heat and cook the chicken, stirring, for 5 minutes or until just cooked through. Remove the chicken from the pan and set aside.

Place 2 tortillas on a board and sprinkle the cheese over them. Top with the chicken, capsicum, jalapeño and coriander. Place the remaining tortillas over the top of each and press down lightly.

Place a clean frying pan over medium–low heat, add the remaining oil and swirl to coat the base of the pan. Place one quesadilla in the pan and cook for 3–5 minutes, then carefully turn it over and cook for another 3 minutes or until the cheese has melted and the quesadilla is golden brown. Repeat with the second quesadilla.

To serve, allow the quesadilla to cool slightly, then cut into wedges, and serve with the salsa and sour cream.

This recipe makes two quesadillas. The second one can be refrigerated, wrapped in plastic wrap, and eaten cold for lunch or as a snack the following day. You can use a bought barbecued chicken to make this a very quick meal. If jalapeños are too spicy, replace with tinned corn.

Beef and cashew noodle salad

500 ml (17 fl oz/2 cups) beef stock
2 tablespoons soy sauce
2 tablespoons lime juice
175 g (6 oz) beef eye fillet
50 g (1¾ oz) dried rice vermicelli noodles
1 tablespoon coriander (cilantro) leaves
1 tablespoon small mint leaves
⅓ long red chilli, seeded and thinly
    sliced lengthways
1 spring onion (scallion), trimmed and
    thinly sliced on an angle
1 small carrot, grated
½ Lebanese (short) cucumber, seeded
    and cut into fine matchsticks
1 tablespoon roasted cashews,
    coarsely chopped

Dressing
1½ tablespoons lime juice
1½ tablespoons fish sauce
1½ tablespoons grated palm
    sugar (jaggery)
2 teaspoons finely grated fresh ginger

To make the dressing, combine all the ingredients in a small bowl and set aside.

Place the stock, soy sauce and lime juice into a saucepan and bring to the boil over medium heat, then add the beef. Reduce the heat to low and cook gently for 5 minutes; do not allow the liquid to boil or the beef will be tough. Remove the meat to a plate, loosely cover with foil and stand for 5 minutes.

Meanwhile, place the noodles in a bowl, pour over hot water to cover, then stand for 5 minutes or until the noodles are soft. Drain well, rinse under cold water, then drain again.

Combine the herbs, chilli, spring onion, carrot, cucumber and noodles in a serving bowl. Slice the beef into 2 mm (1/16 inch) thick slices, then add to the salad.

Drizzle the dressing over the salad and toss to combine. Sprinkle with the cashews and serve.

★ **Preparation time:** 10 minutes   ★ **Cooking time:** 10 minutes   ★ **Serves:** 1

Garlicky white bean brandade

1 teaspoon olive oil
1 small onion, finely chopped
½ teaspoon finely chopped
  rosemary
1 small garlic clove, chopped
1 x 400 g (14 oz) tin white beans,
  rinsed and drained
2–3 anchovy fillets (depending
  on size), drained
1½ tablespoons finely grated
  parmesan cheese
1 tablespoon extra virgin olive oil
4 asparagus spears, trimmed
2 prosciutto slices, torn or cut in
  half lengthways
toasted baguette, to serve

Heat the olive oil in a small non-stick frying pan over a medium–low heat. Add the onion and cook, stirring, for 3 minutes or until translucent. Stir in the rosemary and garlic and cook for 30 seconds.

Transfer to the bowl of a food processor along with the white beans, anchovies, parmesan and 2 tablespoons water. Process until almost smooth. Add the extra virgin olive oil and process again. Season to taste with sea salt and freshly ground black pepper.

Cook the asparagus in a small saucepan of salted boiling water for 2–3 minutes or until tender. Drain and refresh under cold water.

Wrap each asparagus spear in a piece of prosciutto. Serve half of the brandade with the asparagus and toasted baguette on the side.

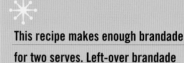

This recipe makes enough brandade for two serves. Left-over brandade will keep in an airtight container in the refrigerator for up to 5 days and is delicious served with chargrilled fish.

Prawn and bok choy omelette

This omelette is also delicious using shredded cooked chicken instead of the prawns.

25 g (1 oz) dried rice vermicelli
2 teaspoons peanut oil
1 head baby bok choy (pak choy), thinly sliced
1 garlic clove, crushed
¼ teaspoon sesame oil
5 raw king prawns (shrimp), peeled, cleaned and coarsely chopped
½ teaspoon soy sauce
2 eggs, lightly beaten
1 tablespoon coconut milk
1 small handful coriander (cilantro) leaves, shredded (optional)
1 sliced red chilli, to serve

Place the vermicelli in a heatproof bowl. Pour over boiling water, cover and stand for 5–10 minutes or until tender. Drain and set aside to keep warm.

Heat 1 teaspoon of the peanut oil in a small ovenproof non-stick frying pan over a medium heat. Add the bok choy, garlic, sesame oil and prawns. Cook, tossing, for 1–2 minutes or until the bok choy has wilted and the prawns are pink. Remove to a bowl and toss through the noodles.

Heat the grill (broiler) to medium–high. Whisk the soy sauce, eggs and coconut milk together. Place the remaining oil in the pan over medium heat. Pour in the egg mixture and arrange the noodle mixture evenly over the top. Cook for 2–3 minutes before transferring to the grill. Grill for a further 2 minutes or until the egg is set.

To serve, slide onto a plate and top with coriander leaves, if using. Sprinkle chilli slices over the top and serve immediately.

Preparation time: 20 minutes   **Cooking time:** 50 minutes   **Serves:** 1

Spicy capsicum and tomato bake with egg

2 tablespoons olive oil

1 small red onion, cut into thin wedges

1 small red capsicum (pepper), seeded and thinly sliced

1 small yellow or orange capsicum (pepper), seeded and thinly sliced

1 garlic clove, crushed

1 scant teaspoon ground cumin

pinch of paprika

2 tomatoes, roughly chopped

2 teaspoons tomato paste (concentrated purée)

50 g (1¾ oz/⅓ cup) tinned cannellini beans, rinsed and drained

1½ tablespoons finely chopped flat-leaf (Italian) parsley

1 egg

toasted Turkish or pitta bread, to serve

Preheat the oven to 180°C (350°F/Gas 4).

Heat the oil in a frying pan over low heat. Add the onion, capsicum and garlic, and cook, stirring, for 15 minutes or until very soft.

Add the cumin and paprika, and cook, stirring, for 1 minute or until fragrant. Add the tomato, tomato paste and 2 tablespoons water. Cook, stirring, for 15 minutes or until the tomato is very soft and a sauce has formed. Stir in the cannellini beans. Season to taste with sea salt and freshly ground black pepper, then stir in the parsley.

Spoon the mixture into a 500 ml (17 fl oz/ 2 cup) capacity ovenproof ramekin (dariole mould). Make a well in the centre and break in the egg. Bake uncovered for 15–20 minutes or until the egg is just set. Serve immediately with the toasted Turkish or pitta bread on the side.

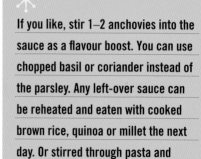

If you like, stir 1–2 anchovies into the sauce as a flavour boost. You can use chopped basil or coriander instead of the parsley. Any left-over sauce can be reheated and eaten with cooked brown rice, quinoa or millet the next day. Or stirred through pasta and served with lots of parmesan.

Lamb, barley and mint salad

55 g (2 oz/¼ cup) pearl barley
150 g (5½ oz) lamb back
   strap, trimmed
1½ tablespoons extra virgin olive oil
2 teaspoons red wine vinegar
1 teaspoon sumac
90 g (3¼ oz/½ cup) seedless red or
   green grapes, halved lengthways
small handful baby rocket (arugula)
2 tablespoons mint
50 g (1¾ oz/⅓ cup) feta cheese

Place the barley in a small saucepan and add enough cold water to cover. Bring to the boil over medium heat, then reduce the heat to medium–low and cook covered for 35 minutes or until tender. Drain well, then place in a bowl.

Meanwhile heat a chargrill pan or small, heavy-based frying pan over medium–high heat. Brush the lamb with about 2 teaspoons of the oil, season to taste with sea salt and freshly ground black pepper, then grill for about 3 minutes on each side or until cooked but still a little pink in the middle. Transfer the lamb to a plate and cool to room temperature.
To make the dressing, whisk together remaining olive oil, vinegar and sumac. Season to taste.

Cut the lamb on the diagonal into 5 mm (¼ inch) thick slices, then add to the barley in the bowl. Add the grapes, rocket and mint, and toss gently to combine. Place salad in a serving bowl and crumble the feta over. Serve with the sumac dressing passed separately.

❋ Preparation time: 5 minutes **❋ Cooking time:** 15 minutes **❋ Serves:** 1

Ravioli with zucchini, sage and pine nuts

150 g (5½ oz/2 cups) ready-made fresh
   chicken ravioli
1 tablespoon butter
1 bacon slice, cut widthways
   into thin strips
1 tablespoon pine nuts
6 sage leaves, torn
1 zucchini (courgette), trimmed and
   thinly sliced
1 tablespoon lemon juice
1 small handful baby spinach leaves
shaved parmesan, to serve

Bring a saucepan of salted water to the boil.
Add the ravioli and cook according to the packet
instructions. Drain and set aside.

Meanwhile, melt the butter in a small frying
pan over medium heat. Add the bacon, pine nuts
and sage and cook for 2 minutes or until the
bacon is crispy. Add the zucchini and lemon juice
and cook, tossing occasionally, until the liquid
has evaporated. Add the ravioli to the pan, add
the spinach and toss until well combined. Season
to taste with sea salt and freshly ground black
pepper and sprinkle with the shaved parmesan.
Serve immediately.

Individual fondue

butter, for greasing
150 g (5½ oz) 'dolce' provolone cheese,
  coarsely grated
½ small baguette, torn into small chunks
1 carrot, cut into matchsticks
50 g (1¾ oz/⅓ cup) cornichons
5 or 6 salami slices
½ small granny smith apple, cored
  and thinly sliced

Preheat the oven to 170°C (325°F/Gas 3).

Using the butter lightly grease the base
and side of a 250 ml (9 fl oz/1 cup) capacity
gratin dish or other small, shallow baking dish,
then place the provolone in the dish. Bake for
10 minutes or until the cheese has melted.

Meanwhile, arrange the remaining ingredients
on a small platter or plate.

Remove the cheese from the oven and
serve immediately with the accompaniments
for scooping up the cheese.

Preparation time: 10 minutes   **Cooking time:** 10 minutes   **Serves:** 1

Preparation time: 15 minutes   **Cooking time:** 10 minutes   **Serves:** 1

Smoked salmon and chargrilled vegetable panzanella

1 small red onion, halved and cut into
   5 mm (¼ inch) thick wedges
½ small red capsicum (pepper), seeded
   and cut into 1.5 cm (⅝ inch) wide strips
1½ tablespoons extra virgin olive oil
50 g (1¾ oz) day-old Italian-style
   bread such as ciabatta (about two
   2 cm/¾ inch wide slices), cut into
   1.5 cm (⅝ inch) pieces
1 very ripe tomato, trimmed and cut into
   1 cm (½ inch) pieces
1 heaped tablespoon pitted green olives
1 small garlic clove, crushed
2½ teaspoons balsamic vinegar
2 tablespoons small basil leaves
2 tablespoons flat-leaf (Italian)
   parsley leaves
125 g (4½ oz) piece hot smoked salmon
   or trout, skin and bones removed, and
   coarsely flaked

Heat a chargrill pan over medium heat. Place the onion and capsicum in a small bowl with ½ tablespoon of the oil and toss to combine well. Place the vegetables in the chargrill pan and cook for 3–4 minutes on each side or until charred and tender. Remove to a plate and cool. Combine the grilled vegetables, bread, tomato, olives, garlic, vinegar and the remaining oil in a bowl and toss to combine well.

Season to taste with sea salt and freshly ground black pepper, then add the remaining ingredients and toss gently to combine. Pile into a bowl and serve immediately.

Lamb burger with hummus and beetroot

The extra lamb patty will keep refrigerated in an airtight container for 2–3 days. Use it for a quick lunch on the run.

350 g (12 oz) minced (ground) lamb
1 teaspoon ground cinnamon
½ small red onion, finely chopped
1½ tablespoons currants
2 tablespoons chopped mint
35 g (1¼ oz/¼ cup) crumbled
  feta cheese
1 garlic clove, crushed
125 g (4½ oz) tin chickpeas (garbanzo
  beans), rinsed and drained
1 tablespoon lemon juice
1 tablespoon extra virgin olive oil
1 tablespoon tahini
1 tablespoon vegetable oil
2 x 8 cm (3¼ inch) long pieces
  Turkish bread
1 small handful rocket (arugula)
225 g (8 oz) tin beetroot
  (beets) slices, drained

Combine the lamb mince, cinnamon, onion, currants, mint, feta and half the garlic in a bowl. Season to taste with sea salt and freshly ground black pepper, then stir to mix well.

To make the hummus, place the remaining garlic, chickpeas, lemon juice, olive oil and tahini in a food processor and process until a smooth paste forms, adding up to 1 tablespoon of water to moisten, if necessary. Season to taste and set aside.

Divide the lamb mixture in half and form each half into a patty about 7 cm (2¾ inches) in diameter. Heat the vegetable oil in a small heavy-based frying pan over a medium–low heat, add the patties and cook for 10 minutes, turning once, or until golden and cooked through.

Slice the Turkish bread in half horizontally and toast. Top one half with the rocket, a lamb patty, a slice of beetroot and some hummus. Serve immediately.

Preparation time: 20 minutes   **Cooking time:** 10 minutes   **Serves:** 1 + 1

Preparation time: 15 minutes   Cooking time: 15 minutes   Serves: 1

Roast asparagus and tofu salad with sesame dressing

1 tablespoon plain (all-purpose) flour
150 g (5½ oz) firm tofu, cut into
  2 cm (¾ inch) pieces
4 thick asparagus spears, trimmed
olive oil spray
1 small handful watercress sprigs
½ avocado, sliced
1 tablespoon finely shredded nori
  (about ¼ sheet), for garnish

Sesame dressing
1 teaspoon tamari or soy sauce
1 teaspoon sesame oil
1 teaspoon Japanese rice vinegar
2 teaspoons toasted sesame seeds

Preheat the oven to 200°C (400°F/Gas 6). Line a baking tray with foil.

To make the sesame dressing, combine the tamari, sesame oil, rice vinegar and 1 tablespoon water in a small bowl and whisk to combine well. Stir in the sesame seeds, then set aside.

Season the flour with sea salt and freshly ground black pepper. Toss the tofu lightly in the flour, shaking off any excess. Place the asparagus and tofu on the baking tray. Spray with the oil to coat all sides of the asparagus and tofu, then roast for 12–15 minutes or until the asparagus is tender and the tofu has a crisp crust.

Place the watercress on a serving plate. Top with the asparagus and tofu, add the avocado slices, then drizzle with the dressing, sprinkle with the nori and serve immediately.

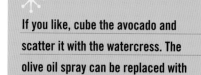

If you like, cube the avocado and scatter it with the watercress. The olive oil spray can be replaced with 2 tablespoons of olive oil. Toss the asparagus and tofu in oil to coat well before roasting.

Smoked chicken Waldorf salad on bruschetta

Prepare the apple just prior to mixing it in with the other ingredients and dressing, or it will go brown. This recipe makes one substantial serve or two smaller ones. Any left-over salad can be refrigerated in an airtight container and eaten the next day. It's also delicious with half an avocado, chopped into 2 cm (¾ inch) cubes, gently folded in just before serving.

2 tablespoons chopped walnuts
  or pecans
4 baguette, ciabatta or sourdough
  bread slices
olive oil, for brushing
½ garlic clove
1 small smoked chicken breast (about
  180 g/6 oz), shredded
½ small red apple, cored and cut into
  1 cm (½ inch) pieces
¼ celery stick, cut into 1 cm
  (½ inch) pieces
1 spring onion (scallion), trimmed
  and chopped
50 g (1¾ oz) small seedless green
  grapes, halved
1 tablespoon chopped flat-leaf
  (Italian) parsley

Dressing
2 tablespoons whole-egg mayonnaise
1 teaspoon white wine vinegar
  or lemon juice
1 teaspoon dijon mustard

To make the dressing, combine all the ingredients in a small bowl, add 2 teaspoons hot water, then whisk until combined. Cover and set aside until needed.

Toast the walnuts or pecans in a frying pan over a medium–low heat, shaking the pan often, for 2–3 minutes or until lightly browned. Cool and chop coarsely.

Preheat the grill (broiler) to medium–high. Brush the bread with olive oil, then rub the bread all over with the garlic. Grill the bread for 1–2 minutes on each side or until lightly golden.

Combine the chicken, apple, celery, spring onion, grapes, parsley and walnuts or pecans in a small bowl and stir to mix well. Season to taste with sea salt and freshly ground black pepper. Add the dressing and toss to combine, then pile the mixture onto the toasted bread and serve immediately.

Preparation time: 15 minutes   **Cooking time:** 5 minutes   **Serves:** 1

✳ **Preparation time:** 15 minutes   ✳ **Cooking time:** 25 minutes   ✳ **Serves:** 1

Tuna Niçoise salad

1 egg

2 kipfler or other small potatoes, peeled

50 g (1¾ oz) baby green beans (about
   12 beans), trimmed

150 g (5½ oz) tuna fillet

olive oil, for cooking

1 small handful baby cos (romaine)
   lettuce leaves

4 cherry tomatoes, halved

6 pitted black olives (about 1 tablespoon)

1 teaspoon drained capers

Dressing

2 teaspoons olive oil

½ teaspoon red wine vinegar

¼ teaspoon dijon mustard

½ garlic clove, crushed

½ anchovy fillet, drained and chopped

Put the egg in a small saucepan of cold water, slowly bring to the boil and cook for 5 minutes. Drain well, then run the egg under cold water to cool. Peel the egg, then set aside.

Cook the potatoes in a small saucepan of boiling salted water for about 15 minutes or until nearly tender. Add the beans and cook for 2–3 minutes or until the beans are tender and the potatoes are cooked through. Drain well, then cool the vegetables. Cut the potatoes into 2.5 cm (1 inch) pieces.

Heat a chargrill pan or a small heavy-based frying pan over a medium–high heat. Brush the tuna fillet lightly with oil, then chargrill or sear the tuna in the pan for 1 minute on each side or until golden on the outside but still quite pink in the middle; take care not to overcook the tuna or it will be dry. Cool to room temperature, then flake the tuna.

To make the dressing, place all the ingredients with a pinch of sugar in a bowl and whisk to combine well. Cut the egg into quarters.

Combine the cos leaves, tomatoes, olives, capers, potatoes and beans in a serving bowl. Scatter over the tuna and egg, drizzle with the dressing and serve immediately.

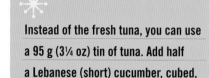

Instead of the fresh tuna, you can use a 95 g (3¼ oz) tin of tuna. Add half a Lebanese (short) cucumber, cubed, if you like. Use a ready-made salad dressing, if you prefer.

BBQ duck and hoisin wrap

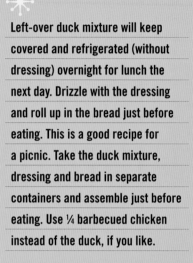

½ Chinese barbecued duck
60 g (2¼ oz/¼ cup) whole-egg mayonnaise
1½ tablespoons hoisin sauce
1 teaspoon sweet chilli sauce
35 g (1¼ oz/¾ cup) finely shredded Chinese cabbage
½ Lebanese (short) cucumber, peeled, seeded and cut very thinly on the diagonal
½ carrot, peeled and cut very thinly on the diagonal
6 cherry tomatoes, quartered
1 spring onion (scallion), finely chopped
1 small handful mung beans, trimmed
1 small handful coriander (cilantro) leaves, chopped
2 pieces flat 'mountain' bread

Remove the duck meat from the bones, discarding any fat and skin, then shred the meat, using your fingers. Place in a bowl and set aside.

In a small bowl combine the mayonnaise, hoisin sauce and sweet chilli sauce.

Add the cabbage, cucumber, carrot and tomato to the shredded duck and toss to combine well. Add the spring onion, mung beans and coriander and toss to combine well.

Divide the mixture between two mountain breads, placing it in an even line at one end. Drizzle with the dressing, then roll the bread up firmly, tucking in the filling as you go. Wrap a strip of foil or baking paper around the centre or tie them up with some string, if you like, to hold them securely together, then serve.

☀ **Preparation time:** 20 minutes   ☀ **Cooking time:** nil   ☀ **Serves:** 1 + 1

❋ **Preparation time:** 10 minutes ❋ **Cooking time:** 15 minutes ❋ **Serves:** 1

Caramel tofu with peanuts and ginger

175 g (6 oz) firm tofu
2 tablespoons caster (superfine) sugar
2 teaspoons fish sauce
2 teaspoons soy sauce
1 cm (½ inch) piece ginger, finely grated
1 cm (½ inch) piece galangal, finely
  grated (optional)
1 small garlic clove, very thinly sliced
½ star anise
steamed bok choy (pak choy)
few sprigs of coriander (cilantro)
1½ tablespoons blanched roasted
  peanuts and steamed rice, to serve

Cut the tofu into 3 cm (1¼ inch) cubes,
then set aside.

Combine the sugar and 2 tablespoons water
in a small frying pan over medium heat. Cook
the mixture, shaking the pan occasionally, for
5 minutes or until it is a deep caramel colour.
Working quickly and taking care as the mixture
will spit, remove the pan from the heat, then
add 80 ml (2½ fl oz/⅓ cup) water, the fish
sauce, soy sauce, ginger, galangal, if using, garlic
and star anise. Return the pan to the heat and
cook over a medium–low heat for 1 minute or
until it boils gently and is smooth.

Add the tofu to the pan and cook for
5–6 minutes, turning once, or until the tofu
is a deep caramel colour and heated through,
and the liquid has reduced. Remove the star
anise. Place the tofu in a serving bowl with the
bok choy, spoon the sauce over, scatter with
the coriander and serve with the peanuts and
steamed rice on the side.

Pastrami and fontina croque monsieur

2 x 1 cm (½ inch) thick slices
   sourdough bread
2 teaspoons dijon mustard
6 pastrami slices
50 g (1¾ oz) fontina cheese, cut
   into 4 slices
2 teaspoons butter, softened
1 teaspoon wholegrain mustard
1 teaspoon balsamic vinegar
2 teaspoons olive oil
1 small handful spinach leaves
1 gherkin, thinly sliced

Lay the bread on a board and cover one side of each slice with mustard. Layer with the pastrami and cheese and sandwich the bread together. Butter the outside of both bread slices and cook in a sandwich maker or a large frying pan over medium heat for 6–8 minutes (turning if using a frying pan) or until golden and the cheese has melted.

Whisk the wholegrain mustard and vinegar in a small bowl, then gradually whisk in the oil to make a dressing. Toss the spinach and gherkin together and drizzle with the salad dressing. Serve the croque monsieur with the salad on the side.

✳ Preparation time: 5 minutes   **✳ Cooking time:** 10 minutes   **✳ Serves:** 1

❋ **Preparation time:** 10 minutes   ❋ **Cooking time:** 35 minutes   ❋ **Serves:** 1

Lamb, lemon and rice soup

3 teaspoons olive oil, plus extra,
  for drizzling
½ small onion, chopped
1 small desiree potato, peeled and
  cut into 1 cm (½ inch) pieces
1 small garlic clove, crushed
50 g (1¾ oz/¼ cup) medium-grain rice
large pinch ground allspice
½ teaspoon dried mint
375 ml (13 fl oz/1½ cups) chicken stock
1 large handful baby spinach leaves
150 g (5½ oz) lamb fillets
  (about 2), trimmed and cut
  into 1 cm (½ inch) pieces
2 teaspoons lemon juice, or to taste
Greek-style yoghurt and lemon wedges,
  to serve

Heat the oil in a small saucepan over medium heat. Add the onion, potato and garlic and cook, stirring, for 5 minutes or until the vegetables have started to soften. Add the rice, allspice, mint, 375 ml (13 fl oz/1½ cups) water and the stock, then bring the mixture to a gentle boil.

Reduce the heat to low, partially cover the pan and cook for 20 minutes or until the rice and potato are very tender. Stir in the spinach, lamb and lemon juice, season to taste with sea salt and freshly ground black pepper, then cook for 3–4 minutes or until the lamb is just cooked but still a little pink in the middle.

Serve the soup immediately in a large bowl with a drizzle of olive oil and lemon wedges, and the yoghurt on the side.

Smoked fish rarebit

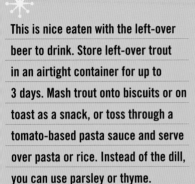

2 thick slices rustic-style bread
  such as ciabatta
¾ tablespoon butter
large pinch dry mustard
1 teaspoon plain (all-purpose) flour
1 tablespoon beer
2 tablespoons grated mature
  cheddar cheese
2 small brussels sprouts, trimmed and
  sliced lengthways into 4 pieces each
3 cherry tomatoes, halved
1 teaspoon chopped dill
1 teaspoon lemon juice
75 g (2¾ oz) hot smoked salmon or trout,
  bones and skin removed, flaked

Preheat the grill (broiler) and lightly toast the bread on both sides. Remove the toast but keep the grill on.

Melt half the butter in a small saucepan over medium heat, add the mustard and flour, and stir until smooth. Add the beer and cheese, reduce the heat to low and cook for about 30 seconds or just until the cheese has melted; take care not to overcook or the mixture will be tough. Remove from the heat.

Heat the remaining butter in a small frying pan over medium heat. Add the brussels sprouts and cook, tossing occasionally, for 2–3 minutes or until softened slightly, then add the tomatoes and dill. Stir in the lemon juice and continue to cook, stirring, for 1 minute or until softened.

Divide the fish and brussels sprout mixture among the toasted slices, then spoon the cheese mixture over, spreading to cover. Transfer to a baking tray and place under the grill for about 1 minute or until hot and bubbling. Serve immediately.

Preparation time: 15 minutes   **Cooking time:** 10 minutes   **Serves:** 1

Mains

Crisp-skin blue eye trevalla with potatoes and red coleslaw • Herbed lamb cutlets with steamed greens and tapénade • Chargrilled piri-piri spatchcock • Vietnamese lemongrass beef stir-fry • Farfalle with tuna, capers and lemon cream sauce • Italian-style beef with vegetables • Mini lamb roast • Quick chicken and mushroom pie • Whole fish steamed with Chinese flavours • Poached chicken and artichoke salad with saffron aïoli • Chinese roast pork with orange sauce • Lamb fillets with zucchini fritters and tahini sauce • Pasta with Italian sausages and balsamic glaze • Veal cutlet with parsnip mash and fig salad • Sweet potato and tofu laksa • Salmon with mango-avocado salsa • Easy beef fajitas • Fillet steak with blue cheese butter and cauliflower crush • Trout in prosciutto with fennel salad • Malay-style chicken curry • Lamb steak with pecorino mash and artichokes • Chilli, chicken and cashew stir-fry • Poached beef with horseradish cream • Roast pork with honey and pomegranate carrots • Yoghurt chicken with Indian spices • Paprika fish with warm potato salad • Chinese poached chicken with bok choy • Pork sausages with cabbage caraway braise • Five-spice lamb and sugarsnap stir-fry • Spatchcock with apricot couscous and zucchini • Individual seafood and tarragon pies • Red flannel hash • Minute steak with brandy cream • Chicken ravioli with lemon burnt butter

Preparation time: 10 minutes   **Cooking time:** 20 minutes   **Serves:** 1

Crisp-skin blue eye trevalla with potatoes and red coleslaw

½ teaspoon wholegrain mustard
1 teaspoon mayonnaise
1 teaspoon sour cream
1 teaspoon orange juice
1 teaspoon red wine vinegar
50 g (1¾ oz/⅔ cup) finely shredded
  red cabbage
1 small beetroot (beet), peeled and grated
1 small red onion, peeled and
  thinly sliced
2 tablespoons chopped parsley
1 tablespoon olive oil
3 new potatoes, very thinly sliced
160 g (5¾ oz) blue eye trevalla
  fillet, skin on

Place the mustard, mayonnaise, sour cream, orange juice and vinegar in a small bowl and whisk to combine well. Combine the cabbage, beetroot, onion and parsley in a bowl. Add the dressing, season to taste with sea salt and freshly ground black pepper and toss to combine well.

Heat the oil in a small frying pan over a medium–high heat. Add the potato slices, in batches if necessary, and cook in a single layer for 5 minutes on each side or until crisp. Remove to paper towels, reserving the pan, to drain excess oil. Place the fish, skin side down, in the pan, then cook over medium heat for 4 minutes or until the skin is golden. Turn, season well, then cook for another 3 minutes or until the fish is cooked through. Serve the fish with the coleslaw and crisp potatoes.

Herbed lamb cutlets with steamed greens and tapénade

To save time, crumb a few extra cutlets and freeze them for another meal.

40 g (1½ oz/½ cup) fresh breadcrumbs
2 tablespoons finely chopped parsley
1 tablespoon finely chopped
    oregano
plain (all-purpose) flour, for dusting
1 egg, beaten
2 lamb cutlets
50 ml (1½ fl oz) olive oil, plus extra,
    for drizzling
80 g baby green beans, cut in
    half diagonally
35 g (1¼ oz) frozen peas
40 g (1½ oz/¼ cup) frozen broad
    (fava) beans
1 tablespoon mint leaves
1 tablespoon ready-made tapénade

Combine the breadcrumbs, parsley and oregano in a shallow bowl. Place the flour in another shallow bowl and season with sea salt and freshly ground black pepper. Place the egg in a third bowl, add 1 tablespoon cold water and stir to combine well.

Dip each cutlet into the flour, shaking off any excess, then into the egg mixture and finally into the breadcrumb mixture, lightly pressing to coat well. Place onto a baking paper-lined baking tray and refrigerate for 15–20 minutes to firm the coating.

Heat the oil in a frying pan over a medium–low heat and when hot, add cutlets and cook for 3 minutes each side or until golden and the meat is cooked to your liking. Drain the cutlets on paper towels to remove excess oil.

Meanwhile, bring a saucepan of salted water to the boil over medium heat, add the beans and cook for 2 minutes, then add the peas and broad beans and cook for a further minute or until the vegetables are tender. Drain well, then peel the outer shell of the broad beans.

To serve, place the greens on a plate, top with the cutlets, scatter with the mint leaves, drizzle with olive oil and serve with the tapénade on the side.

✳ **Preparation time:** 15 minutes, plus 20 minutes chilling   ✳ **Cooking time:** 10 minutes   ✳ **Serves:** 1

81   SINGLE SERVES

Preparation time: 15 minutes, plus 4 hours marinating time

Cooking time: 40 minutes

Serves: 1

Chargrilled piri-piri spatchcock

2 teaspoons chilli flakes
  or to taste, roasted
2 garlic cloves or to taste, crushed
1 tablespoon paprika
60 ml (2 fl oz/¼ cup) lemon juice
1 teaspoon red wine vinegar
80 ml (2½ fl oz/⅓ cup) olive oil, plus
  extra, for cooking
2 tablespoons coriander (cilantro)
  leaves, chopped
1 spatchcock
1 lemon, halved
steamed new potatoes and baby green
  beans, to serve

Place the chilli flakes, garlic, paprika, lemon juice, vinegar and olive oil in a bowl and stir to combine well. Stir in the coriander.

Rinse the spatchcock, then pat dry with paper towels. Place the spatchcock, breast side down, on a board. Using a pair of sharp kitchen scissors, cut down both sides of the backbone, then discard the bone. Open the spatchcock up, flattening it with the heel of your hand. Place it in a bowl, spoon half the marinade over, then rub it in well. Cover and refrigerate for 4 hours or overnight.

Heat a chargrill pan over a medium–low heat. Drain the spatchcock well, reserving the marinade, then brush with the extra oil and grill, skin side down, for 20 minutes, brushing occasionally with the reserved marinade. Turn the spatchcock, then cover with foil or a lid and cook, brushing occasionally with the marinade, for another 15–20 minutes, or until cooked through and the skin is well charred. While the spatchcock is cooking, place the lemon, cut side down, onto the chargrill pan, and cook for 3 minutes or until the surface is charred. (Alternatively the spatchcock can be placed onto a tray, and cooked in a 200°C (400°F/ Gas 6) oven for 30 minutes until it is golden and cooked when tested, basting with any remaining marinade during cooking.)

Serve with the steamed potatoes, baby beans and charred lemon.

The piri-piri marinade is enough for 2 spatchcocks, so another one can be cooked for a friend. Or you can store the marinade in an airtight container in the fridge for up to 1 month. Instead of dried chilli flakes, you can use 2–3 fresh bird's eye chillies. Roast in a 200°C (400°F/ Gas 6) oven for 10 minutes, then chop finely. Instead of spatchcock, you can use chicken legs or even fillets. For extra flavour, make shallow cuts in the thicker parts of the chicken legs before marinating.

Vietnamese lemongrass beef stir-fry

To make it easier to thinly slice
the meat, freeze it for about 1 hour
beforehand to firm it up. It's best to
have all the ingredients prepared
before cooking begins. A cucumber
and lettuce salad would make a
perfect side dish for this stir-fry.

175 g (6 oz) piece sirloin, skirt or rump
  steak, trimmed and thinly sliced
1 teaspoon cornflour (cornstarch)
1 garlic clove, finely chopped
1 red bird's eye chilli, finely chopped
1 teaspoon chopped ginger
1 lemongrass stem, white part only,
  finely chopped
2 teaspoons fish sauce
2 teaspoons oyster sauce
1½ tablespoons vegetable or peanut oil
½ red onion, cut into thin wedges
½ small carrot, cut into matchsticks
2 teaspoons sugar
roasted unsalted peanuts, roughly
  chopped, to serve
coriander (cilantro) leaves, to serve
steamed rice, to serve

Combine the meat, cornflour, garlic, chilli, ginger, lemongrass, fish sauce and oyster sauce in a small bowl. Cover and refrigerate for 20 minutes or until ready to cook.

Heat a wok or frying pan over medium heat until it begins to smoke, then add half the oil. Add the onion and carrot and stir-fry for 1 minute or until softened slightly, then transfer to a bowl.

Wipe the wok clean, add the remaining oil, return the wok to the heat and when hot, stir-fry the prepared meat mixture, tossing for 2 minutes or until meat is browned but still a little pink in the middle. Return the vegetables to the wok, add the sugar and toss for 1 minute to combine. To serve, place the stir-fry onto a serving dish, garnish with peanuts and coriander and serve with the steamed rice on the side.

❋ **Preparation time:** 15 minutes,
plus 20 minutes marinating time

❋ **Cooking time:** 5 minutes

❋ **Serves:** 1

Preparation time: 10 minutes   **Cooking time:** 15 minutes   **Serves:** 1

Farfalle with tuna, capers and lemon cream sauce

165 g (5¾ oz) tuna fillet, trimmed
65 g (2½ oz/¾ cup) farfalle pasta
60 ml (2 fl oz/¼ cup) cream
handful baby rocket (arugula)
2½ teaspoons small capers, drained
½ teaspoon finely grated lemon rind
2½ teaspoons lemon juice
pinch dried chilli flakes (optional)

Using a large, sharp knife, cut the tuna into 1 cm (½ inch) pieces and set aside.

Cook the pasta in boiling, salted water for 13 minutes or according to packet instructions until al dente. Drain well.

Meanwhile, combine the cream, rocket and capers in a small saucepan or frying pan over a medium–low heat, cover and bring to a gentle boil. Add the lemon rind and stir to combine well, then cook for 1 minute or until the rocket is just wilted. Add the tuna, lemon juice and pasta to the pan, toss to combine well and heat for 30–40 seconds to warm the tuna through. Season to taste with sea salt, freshly ground black pepper and chilli flakes, if using. Serve immediately.

Use the freshest tuna you can find. If you like your tuna cooked all the way through, add it to the pan sooner so it cooks for longer. You can also use fresh or smoked salmon or trout; if using smoked fish, use about 50 g (1¾ oz) less.

Italian-style beef with vegetables

½ red onion, cut into 6 wedges
200 g (7 oz) piece butternut pumpkin, (squash) peeled and cut into 1 cm (½ inch) thick wedges
2 tablespoons olive oil
160 g (5¾ oz) beef eye fillet, trimmed
1 tablespoon small basil leaves
1 tablespoon shaved parmesan
1 tablespoon pine nuts, toasted
2 tablespoons extra virgin olive oil
1 teaspoon white wine vinegar
1 small garlic clove, crushed
pinch caster (superfine) sugar

Preheat the oven to 200°C (400°F/Gas 6).

Combine the onion, pumpkin and half the oil on a small baking tray, turning to coat the vegetables in the oil. Season to taste with sea salt and freshly ground black pepper, then roast for 15 minutes or until half-cooked.

Meanwhile, using kitchen string, tie the eye fillet firmly around the middle to form a neat shape. Heat the remaining oil in a small heavy-based frying pan over high heat until very hot. Season the steak and add to the pan. Cook for 1 minute on each side to seal, then add to the vegetables in the oven. Bake for 10–15 minutes for medium (depending on thickness of the steak), then remove the steak to a plate, cover with foil and keep warm. Cook the vegetables for a further 5 minutes, if necessary, or turn off the oven and keep warm.

Combine the remaining ingredients in a bowl and stir to mix well. Remove the string from the steak. Place the vegetables on a warmed plate, top with the steak, then scatter over the basil mixture and serve immediately.

Preparation time: 15 minutes   **Cooking time:** 35 minutes   **Serves:** 1

Preparation time: 15 minutes **Cooking time:** 55 minutes **Serves:** 1 + 1

Mini lamb roast

3 teaspoons olive oil
400 g (14 oz) boneless lamb
  mini roast (rump)
1 garlic clove, cut into slivers
1 teaspoon rosemary
3 new potatoes
250 g (9 oz) pumpkin (winter squash),
  cut into 5 cm (2 inch) pieces
1 carrot, halved lengthways
1 parsnip, quartered lengthways
1 small fennel bulb, trimmed and halved
1 small red onion, halved
125 ml (4 fl oz /½ cup) chicken or
  vegetable stock
60 ml (2 fl oz /¼ cup) red wine
2 teaspoons butter, softened
2 teaspoons plain (all-purpose) flour
cooked baby peas, to serve
mint jelly, to serve

Preheat the oven to 200°C (400°F/Gas 6).

Place the oil in a large bowl. Using a small sharp knife, make several incisions in the lamb and insert the garlic and rosemary into the cuts. Brush the lamb with a little of the oil, then season to taste with sea salt and freshly ground black pepper and place in a roasting tin.

Add the prepared vegetables to the remaining oil in the bowl. Using clean hands, rub the vegetables to lightly coat with the oil, season to taste, then arrange around the lamb in the tin. Bake for 35 minutes or until the lamb is cooked but still a little pink in the middle.

Transfer the lamb to a plate, cover loosely with foil and leave to rest in a warm place. Bake the vegetables for a further 15 minutes, or until tender. Remove to a dish and keep warm.

Pour roasting juices and any meat and vegetable sediment into a saucepan, add the stock and red wine and stir over medium heat until the meat and vegetable sediment is incorporated. Bring to the boil. In a small dish, blend the butter and flour until well combined, then whisk into the boiling liquid. Reduce the heat to low and cook, stirring constantly, for 3 minutes. Season to taste.

Serve the lamb and roast vegetables with the gravy, cooked peas and mint jelly on the side.

Take the lamb out of the refrigerator 15–20 minutes before roasting. Use any left-over lamb to make a salad the next day. Place rocket (arugula), strips of lamb, finely shaved red onion, halved cherry tomatoes and a few pine nuts in a shallow bowl. Drizzle with extra virgin olive oil and a little balsamic vinegar and top with crumbled feta or goat's cheese.

Quick chicken and mushroom pie

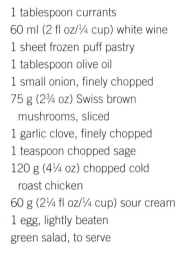

1 tablespoon currants
60 ml (2 fl oz/¼ cup) white wine
1 sheet frozen puff pastry
1 tablespoon olive oil
1 small onion, finely chopped
75 g (2¾ oz) Swiss brown
   mushrooms, sliced
1 garlic clove, finely chopped
1 teaspoon chopped sage
120 g (4¼ oz) chopped cold
   roast chicken
60 g (2¼ fl oz/¼ cup) sour cream
1 egg, lightly beaten
green salad, to serve

Combine the currants and wine in a small bowl. Leave to soak for 15 minutes.

Meanwhile, preheat the oven to 190°C (375°F/ Gas 5). Invert a 300 ml (10½ fl oz) capacity ceramic baking dish onto the frozen pastry sheet. Leaving a 1 cm (½ inch) extra border, cut around the circumference of the dish, then transfer the pastry disc to a plate, cover and refrigerate until ready to use. Return the remaining frozen pastry to the freezer for another use.

Heat the oil in a heavy-based saucepan over medium heat. Cook the onion for 5 minutes or until softened. Stir in the mushrooms and cook for 5 minutes or until softened. Stir in the garlic and sage, and cook for 1 minute, then add the currants and wine, reduce the heat to low and cook until the liquid is reduced to a tablespoon. Stir in the chicken, sour cream and 1 tablespoon water and bring to a gentle boil to heat the meat through, adding a little extra water if necessary. Season to taste with sea salt and freshly ground black pepper.

Spoon the mixture into the baking dish. Brush the top edge of the dish with egg. Place the disc of pastry over the dish to cover with about 1 centimetre (½ inch) overhanging the edges. Press to seal the pastry to the top edge of the dish. Brush the pastry surface lightly with egg, then using a small sharp knife, make a few slits in the pastry to allow air to escape. Place on a baking tray and bake for 20 minutes or until the pastry is golden brown and puffed. Serve immediately with a green salad.

Preparation time: 10 minutes **Cooking time:** 10 minutes **Serves:** 1

Whole fish steamed with Chinese flavours

400 g (14 oz) whole baby barramundi
  or snapper, cleaned and scaled
1 spring onion (scallion), trimmed
  and finely sliced
1 garlic clove, sliced
1 teaspoon finely sliced fresh ginger
1 tablespoon light soy sauce
2 teaspoons sesame oil
1 teaspoon caster (superfine) sugar
½ teaspoon cornflour (cornstarch)
steamed rice, to serve

Garnish

1 spring onion (scallion), trimmed
  and finely sliced
8 coriander (cilantro) leaves
½ large red chilli, seeded and
  thinly sliced, or to taste

Place a bamboo steamer in a large frying pan or wok, add water to the pan so it comes just to the base of the steamer; the water should not touch the steamer. Bring the water to the boil. Line the steamer with baking paper and place the fish on top of the paper.

Combine the spring onion, garlic, ginger, soy sauce, sesame oil, sugar and cornflour in a small bowl and stir to mix well. Spoon the mixture over the fish, cover and steam for 8–10 minutes or until the fish is just cooked through.

Garnish with the spring onion, coriander and chilli slices and serve with steamed rice on the side.

Poached chicken and artichoke salad with saffron aïoli

small pinch saffron threads
180 g (6 oz) chicken breast fillet
500 ml (17 fl oz/2 cups) chicken stock
2 tablespoons ready-made aïoli
½ teaspoon lemon juice, or to taste
3 kipfler potatoes, unpeeled, boiled
   and sliced
2 marinated artichoke hearts, quartered
3 caperberries, halved
½ teaspoon thyme leaves, chopped
2 teaspoons chopped flat-leaf
   (Italian) parsley
1 small handful baby rocket (arugula)
2 teaspoons olive oil
lemon cheeks, to serve

Place the saffron threads in a small bowl, add 2 teaspoons boiling water and stand for 20 minutes.

Meanwhile, place the chicken and stock in a small saucepan over a medium–low heat. Bring to a gentle boil, then reduce the heat to very low, cover and cook for 8 minutes. Remove the pan from the heat and stand for 15 minutes.

Combine the aïoli, saffron mixture and lemon juice in a small bowl and set aside.

Combine the potato, artichokes, caperberries, thyme, parsley and rocket in a bowl. Remove the chicken from the pan and finely shred or slice on the diagonal, then add to the potato mixture. Drizzle with the olive oil and toss to combine well.

Place the chicken salad in a serving bowl and serve with the saffron aïoli and lemon cheeks on the side.

✳ **Preparation time:** 10 minutes,
plus 20 minutes standing

✳ **Cooking time:** 10 minutes

✳ **Serves:** 1

Preparation time: 15 minutes, plus at least 1 hour marinating

Cooking time: 30 minutes

Serves 1

Chinese roast pork with orange sauce

2 tablespoons hoisin sauce

2 tablespoons brown sugar

1 tablespoon Chinese rice wine

125 ml (4 fl oz/½ cup) orange juice

1 garlic clove, crushed

1 teaspoon sesame oil

1 star anise

2 teaspoons soy sauce

400 g (14 oz) pork fillet
(about 1 large), trimmed

2 teaspoons peanut oil

2 teaspoons fresh ginger, cut
into matchsticks

1 spring onion (scallion), trimmed
and thinly sliced

½ teaspoon cornflour (cornstarch)

steamed rice, to serve

steamed bok choy (pak choy) and
snow peas (mangetout), to serve

Combine the hoisin sauce, sugar, rice wine, orange juice, garlic, sesame oil, star anise and soy sauce in a bowl and mix well. Add the pork fillet, toss to coat, then cover and refrigerate for at least 1 hour.

Preheat the oven to 220°C (425°F/Gas 7). Drain the pork well, reserving the marinade, then place the pork on a wire rack over a roasting tin filled with 3 cm (1¼ inches) water. Roast the pork for 25 minutes or until just cooked through, brushing occasionally with some of the reserved marinade. Remove and transfer the pork to a warm plate. Cover loosely with foil and rest for 10 minutes.

Heat the peanut oil in a small pan over low heat. Add the ginger and spring onion and cook, stirring, for 1 minute or until fragrant. Add the reserved marinade, bring the mixture to the boil, then cook gently for 2–3 minutes. Combine the cornflour in a small bowl or cup with 2 teaspoons water to form a smooth paste. Stirring constantly, add the cornflour to the marinade and cook for 1–2 minutes or until thickened slightly. Remove the star anise and discard.

Slice the pork on the diagonal into 1 cm (½ inch) thick pieces. Place the rice on a plate, top with the pork and steamed vegetables, spoon the sauce over and serve immediately.

The pork can be marinated up to 24 hours ahead. Chop any left-over pork to make fresh spring rolls. Combine pork with kecap manis and place on softened rice-paper wrappers. Top with finely shredded cabbage or lettuce, grated carrot, sliced spring onions (scallions), finely chopped red capsicum (pepper) and cucumber. Roll up and serve with a sweet chilli and light soy dipping sauce.

Lamb fillets with zucchini fritters and tahini sauce

200 g (7 oz/1½ cups) zucchini
 (courgettes), grated (about 2)
1 egg, lightly beaten
½ brown onion, finely chopped
pinch ground nutmeg
35 g (1¼ oz/¼ cup) plain
 (all-purpose) flour
200 g (7 oz) Greek-style yoghurt
1 teaspoon tahini
1 garlic clove, finely chopped
60 ml (2 fl oz/¼ cup) vegetable oil
¼ teaspoon ground cumin
½ teaspoon ground paprika
175 g (6 oz) lamb fillets (about 2 fillets)
100 g (3½ oz) cherry tomatoes, halved
small handful flat-leaf (Italian) parsley
1 teaspoon olive oil

Preheat the oven to 150°C (300°F/Gas 2).

Place the zucchini in a colander, sprinkle lightly with salt, then stand for 1 hour to drain. Squeeze as much liquid as possible from the zucchini and place in a bowl. Add the egg, onion, nutmeg, flour and 2 teaspoons water, season to taste with sea salt and freshly ground black pepper and stir to combine well.

In another bowl combine the yoghurt, tahini and garlic, season to taste and refrigerate until required.

Place 2 tablespoons of the vegetable oil in a frying pan over medium–low heat. When the oil is hot, drop spoonfuls of the zucchini mixture into the pan, forming 7 cm (2¾ inch) patties about 2 cm (¾ inch) thick. Cook for 8 minutes, turning once, or until golden and cooked through. Transfer to a baking tray lined with paper towels, reserving the frying pan, and place in the oven to keep the patties warm.

Combine the cumin, paprika and ½ teaspoon salt in a small bowl. Wipe the reserved frying pan clean, then place over medium heat. Add the remaining vegetable oil to the pan. Sprinkle the lamb fillets with the spice mix, place in the pan and cook, turning occasionally, for 5 minutes or until golden and just cooked through; the lamb should still be a little pink in the middle.

Combine the tomatoes, parsley and oil in a bowl. Cut the lamb fillets into pieces and place on a plate with the tomato salad and the zucchini fritters. Drizzle the fritters with the tahini sauce and serve immediately.

Preparation time: 20 minutes,
plus 1 hour standing

Cooking time: 15 minutes

Serves: 1

Preparation time: 20 minutes **Cooking time:** 25 minutes **Serves:** 1

Pasta with Italian sausages and balsamic glaze

1 tablespoon olive oil
1 red onion, cut into thin wedges
2 garlic cloves, crushed
2 Italian sausages (about 175 g/6 oz), skins removed
2 tablespoons raisins, chopped
1 tablespoon balsamic vinegar
1 teaspoon brown sugar
125 ml (4 fl oz/½ cup) chicken or beef stock
125 ml (4 fl oz/½ cup) red wine
3 teaspoons fresh thyme or 1 teaspoon dried, or to taste, plus a few sprigs to serve
100 g (3½ oz) fettuccine
shaved parmesan and rocket salad, to serve

Place the oil in a frying pan over medium heat, add the onion and garlic and cook, stirring often, for 5 minutes or until softened. Add the sausages, breaking up the meat with a wooden spoon, and cook, stirring, for 3–4 minutes or until the meat changes colour. Add the raisins, vinegar, sugar, stock, red wine and thyme to the pan. Bring the mixture to the boil, then lower the heat and cook for 10–15 minutes, stirring occasionally until the sauce is reduced and thickened.

Meanwhile, cook the pasta in a large saucepan of boiling salted water according to the packet instructions until al dente. Drain well, place in a serving bowl, top with the sauce and serve immediately, garnished with the thyme sprigs and with the shaved parmesan and rocket salad on the side.

Any type of pasta would work well with this recipe. If you like short pasta, try it with penne.

Veal cutlet with parsnip mash and fig salad

2 parsnips, peeled, cored and sliced
125 ml (4 fl oz/½ cup) vegetable stock
¾ tablespoon butter
1 small handful rocket (arugula)
2 dried figs, thinly sliced
25 g (1 oz/¼ cup) toasted walnut
    halves, chopped
2 teaspoons olive oil
200 g (7 oz) veal cutlet, about
    1 cm (½ inch) thick

Chardonnay sauce
1 small French shallot, finely chopped
60 ml (2 fl oz/¼ cup) chardonnay
125 ml (4 fl oz/½ cup) cream
½ tablespoon butter, chopped

Place the parsnips in a small saucepan over medium heat, add the vegetable stock and bring to the boil. Cook for 15 minutes or until soft. Drain the parsnip, reserving the cooking liquid. Measure 1 tablespoon of the liquid and combine with the parsnips and butter in a food processor, discarding the remaining liquid. Process until smooth, then season to taste with sea salt and freshly ground black pepper. Keep warm.

For the salad, combine the rocket, figs, walnuts and oil in a small bowl and toss to combine well. Set aside.

Place a chargrill or frying pan over a medium–high heat, add the veal cutlet and cook 3 minutes on each side or until cooked through but still a little pink in the middle. Remove to a plate, cover loosely with foil and keep warm.

To make the chardonnay sauce, place the shallot and wine in a small saucepan over a medium–low heat. Bring to the boil, reduce the heat to low and cook for 2–3 minutes or until reduced by half. Add the cream, increase the heat to medium, bring to the boil, then reduce the heat to low and cook for 2–3 minutes or until reduced by half. Whisk in the butter.

To serve place a large spoonful of the parsnip mash on the plate, place the cutlet to one side of the mash, then spoon the sauce over. Place the salad on the side and serve immediately.

※ **Preparation time:** 15 minutes ※ **Cooking time:** 30 minutes ※ **Serves:** 1

Preparation time: 15 minutes   **Cooking time:** 20 minutes   **Serves:** 1

Sweet potato and tofu laksa

50 g (1¾ oz/⅓ cup) chopped
  sweet potato
75 g (2½ oz/¾ cup) fresh thin
  rice noodles
2 teaspoons peanut oil
55 g (2 oz) ready-made laksa paste
250 ml (9 fl oz/1 cup) coconut milk
250 ml (9 fl oz/1 cup) chicken or
  vegetable stock or water
2 kaffir lime leaves, shredded (optional)
½ lemongrass stem, trimmed and sliced
  in half lengthways (optional)
5 cherry tomatoes, halved
75 g (2¾ oz) firm tofu, cut into
  2 cm (¾ inch) cubes
2 teaspoons fish sauce
1 teaspoon sweet chilli sauce
1 teaspoon lime juice
50 g (1¾ oz) trimmed snow peas
  (mangetout), halved diagonally
1 small handful coriander (cilantro) leaves
½ medium red chilli, sliced in half,
  seeded and thinly sliced (optional)

Place the sweet potato in a steamer and cook
for 7–10 minutes or until just tender.

Meanwhile, place the noodles in a heatproof
bowl. Pour over boiling water, cover and stand for
5–10 minutes or until tender. Drain and place
into a deep serving bowl.

Heat the oil in a wok over high heat. Add
the paste and cook, stirring, for 30 seconds or
until fragrant.

Pour in the coconut milk, stock or water and
add the lime leaves and lemongrass, if using.
Bring to the boil, reduce the heat to medium and
cook gently for 3 minutes. Add the tomatoes
and cook for 2–3 minutes or until just collapsing.
Stir in the tofu, fish sauce, sweet chilli sauce,
lime juice and snow peas. Cook for 1–2 minutes
or until the tofu has warmed through and the
snow peas are tender. Remove the lime leaves
and lemongrass, if using.

Spoon the laksa over the noodles and top with
the coriander leaves and sliced chilli, if using.
Serve immediately.

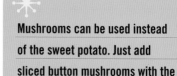

Mushrooms can be used instead
of the sweet potato. Just add
sliced button mushrooms with the
tomatoes. To add extra heat to the
soup, stir a chopped fresh bird's eye
chilli into the curry paste.

Salmon with mango-avocado salsa

Use the left-over salsa the next day for a salad. Place the salsa in a bowl, add 5 peeled king prawns (shrimp), a handful of mixed salad greens and fresh lime juice to taste, toss well and serve.

½ small mango, peeled, seeded and
   cut into 1 cm (½ inch) pieces, or
   60 g (2¼ oz) tinned mango, drained
¼ avocado, cut into 1 cm (½ inch) pieces
1 spring onion (scallion), thinly sliced
   on the diagonal
¼ red capsicum (pepper), seeded and
   cut into 5 mm (¼ inch) pieces
60 ml (2 fl oz/¼ cup) lime juice
2 tablespoons caster (superfine) sugar
1 tablespoon sweet chilli sauce (optional)
1 tablespoon coriander (cilantro) leaves
1 tablespoon plain (all-purpose) flour
½ teaspoon paprika
200 g (7 oz) salmon fillet
150 g (5½ oz) sweet potato (about
   ½ medium one), peeled and cut into
   1 cm (½ inch) rounds
60 ml (2 fl oz/¼ cup) olive oil

Preheat the oven to 180°C (350°F/Gas 4).

Combine the mango, avocado, onion and capsicum in a bowl and set aside. In a saucepan combine the lime juice and sugar and cook over a medium heat for 3–5 minutes or until mixture boils, reduces and thickens slightly. Cool, then pour over the mango mixture and set aside. Add the sweet chilli sauce, if using, and coriander and season to taste with sea salt and freshly ground black pepper.

Combine the flour and paprika on a plate, season to taste and mix well. Dust the salmon in the mixture, shaking off any excess, and set aside. Dust the sweet potato in the flour and shake off any excess.

Heat 1 tablespoon of the oil in a frying pan over medium heat. Add the sweet potato slices and cook for 4 minutes on each side or until golden, then drain on paper towels. Wipe the pan clean, add the remaining oil and place over medium heat. Place the salmon in the pan skin side down and cook for 3 minutes or until the skin is crisp. Turn and cook for 2 minutes or until the salmon is cooked through but still a little pink in the middle.

To serve, place the sweet potato rounds on a plate, top with the salmon, spoon over the mango salsa and serve immediately.

Preparation time: 10 minutes   **Cooking time:** 20 minutes   **Serves:** 1

Easy beef fajitas

1 tablespoon olive oil
1 garlic clove, crushed
½ small bird's eye chilli, thinly sliced
¼ teaspoon dried oregano
¼ teaspoon paprika
¼ teaspoon ground cumin
1 teaspoon lime juice
½ red onion, thinly sliced
¼ red capsicum (pepper), seeded
  and thinly sliced
175 g (6 oz) rump steak, cut into
  thin strips
2 soft flour mini tortillas
1 tomato, thinly sliced
½ avocado, thinly sliced
1 tablespoon coriander (cilantro) leaves
50 g (1¾ oz) mixed lettuce leaves,
  to serve
lime wedges, to serve

Combine the oil, garlic, chilli, oregano, paprika, cumin, lime juice, onion and capsicum in a small bowl and stir to combine well. Add the meat, toss to coat well, then cover and refrigerate for 1 hour.

Heat a frying pan over high heat, add the steak mixture and cook, stirring, for 3–4 minutes or until the meat is cooked but still a little pink in the middle. Cook a little longer if desired.

Place a frying pan over medium heat and when hot, add the tortillas one at a time and cook for 3 minutes or until soft and bubbles appear on the surface.

To serve, divide the steak mixture between the tortillas, then top with the tomato, avocado and coriander. Serve with lettuce leaves and lime wedges on the side.

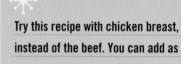

Try this recipe with chicken breast, instead of the beef. You can add as many extra accompaniments as you like such as sour cream, tomato salsa and chopped jalapeños.

Fillet steak with blue cheese butter and cauliflower crush

Use the remaining butter on salmon, chicken or scrambled eggs. It is also great with potatoes or broccoli. The butter will keep refrigerated for up to 4 days and in the freezer for up to 2 months. This recipe also works well with lamb chops.

2 teaspoons butter
1 French shallot, peeled and
  finely chopped
150 g (5½ oz/1¼ cups) small
  cauliflower florets
100 g (3½ oz/½ cup) tinned cannellini
  beans, rinsed and drained
1 tablespoon finely chopped flat-leaf
  (Italian) parsley, plus a few leaves,
  to garnish
olive oil, for cooking
225 g (8 oz) beef eye fillet

Blue cheese butter
50 g butter, softened
1½ tablespoons soft blue cheese
½ garlic clove, very finely chopped
3 teaspoons finely chopped chives

To make the blue cheese butter, combine the butter, cheese and garlic in a small bowl, using a fork, until smooth. Stir in the chives, then place the butter on a piece of plastic wrap and form into a rough log shape about 7 cm (2¾ inches) long. Wrap the butter well in plastic wrap, then using your hands, gently roll it on a work surface until it is a smooth, even roll. Twist the plastic at each end to secure, then freeze for 30 minutes or until firm.

Place the 2 teaspoons butter in a small, heavy-based frying pan over medium heat and cook for 1 minute or until melted and foaming, then add the shallot. Cook for 1 minute, stirring often, then add the cauliflower, cover and cook, stirring occasionally, over a low heat for about 8 minutes or until soft and golden. Season to taste with sea salt and freshly ground black pepper. Add the beans and lightly mash with a fork until a coarse purée forms. Cook over a low heat, stirring, for 1 minute or until the mash is heated through. Stir in the parsley, then cover and keep warm.

Heat a chargrill pan or small heavy-based frying pan over a medium–high heat. Brush the steak all over with the oil, season to taste, then cook for 3–5 minutes on each side depending on thickness, or until cooked to your liking. Remove to a plate, cover loosely with foil and rest for 2 minutes.

To serve, remove the butter from the freezer and cut the log in half, then slice one half into 5 mm (¼ inch) thick pieces; refrigerate the remaining butter for later use. Place the steak and cauliflower mash on a plate, top the steak with the blue cheese butter and serve immediately.

Preparation time: 15 minutes, plus 30 minutes freezing

Cooking time: 20 minutes

Serves: 1

Preparation time: 20 minutes   **Cooking time:** 35 minutes   **Serves:** 1

Trout in prosciutto with fennel salad

2 prosciutto slices
335 g (11¾ oz) baby rainbow trout
2 small desiree potatoes, cut into
  2 cm (¾ inch) pieces
1 rosemary sprig, leaves removed
1 tablespoon butter
1 small orange, peeled
1 small fennel bulb, trimmed and
  thinly sliced
¼ red onion, thinly sliced
1 teaspoon capers
2½ teaspoons extra virgin olive oil
2 tablespoons chopped flat-leaf
  (Italian) parsley

Preheat the oven to 180°C (350°F/Gas 4).

Overlap the prosciutto slices on a board to form a rectangle about 11 x 23 cm (4¼ x 9 inches). Place the trout on the rectangle, then roll the prosciutto around the trout to enclose the middle part of the fish.

Place the potatoes in a roasting tin, sprinkle with the rosemary and dot with the butter, then roast for 15 minutes, turning occasionally.

Add the trout to the baking dish and bake for 20 minutes or until the trout is cooked through and the potatoes are golden. Keep warm.

Meanwhile, using a small, sharp knife and holding the orange over a bowl to collect the juice, cut between the orange membranes to remove the segments. Add the juice to the fish and potatoes in the baking dish.

Combine the fennel, orange segments, onion and capers in a small bowl. Add the oil and toss to coat, then season to taste with sea salt and freshly ground black pepper. Scatter with the parsley.

To serve, place the trout, potatoes and salad on a plate. Drizzle the fish with the pan juices and serve immediately.

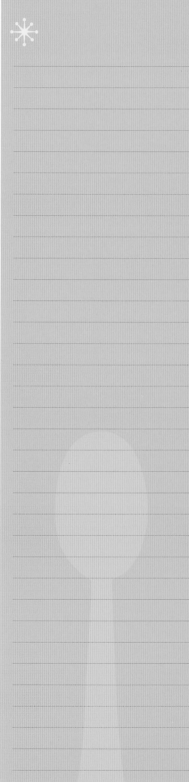

Malay-style chicken curry

This recipe makes 2 serves. Freeze the second portion without any green beans until needed. When reheating the curry, bring to a gentle boil, then add 50 g (1¾ oz/ ⅓ cup) trimmed green beans and cook for 5 minutes. If short on time, omit the lemongrass, curry powder and spice paste and replace with 2 tablespoons of a ready-made curry paste. Stir-fry the paste in the oil until aromatic. Add the chicken, cinnamon and star anise and stir to coat in the paste, then add the coconut milk and tomatoes and continue with the recipe.

2 tablespoons vegetable oil
2 teaspoons Malay curry powder,
 or to taste
400 g (14 oz) chicken thigh
 fillets, trimmed and cut into
 4 cm (1½ inch) pieces
½ cinnamon stick
½ star anise
1 lemongrass stem, trimmed and bruised
165 ml (5½ fl oz) tin coconut milk
400 g (14 oz) tin diced tomatoes
150 g (5¼ oz) sweet potato, peeled
 and cut into 2 cm (¾ inch) pieces
50 g (1¾ oz) green beans, trimmed
2 teaspoons grated palm sugar (jaggery)
2 teaspoons fish sauce
2 teaspoons lime juice
100 g (3½ oz/½ cup) long-grain rice
lime cheek, to serve

Spice paste
1 small onion, roughly chopped
2 cm (¾ inch) piece ginger,
 peeled and chopped
3 garlic cloves

To make the spice paste, blend all the ingredients in a small food processor until a paste-like consistency.

Heat the oil in a saucepan over a medium–low heat. Stir in the spice paste and cook until softened and translucent. Add the curry powder, chicken, cinnamon, star anise and lemongrass. Stir to coat the chicken, then cook for 1–2 minutes or until aromatic. Increase the heat to medium–high, then add the coconut milk, tomato and sweet potato. Season to taste with sea salt, bring to the boil, then reduce the heat to low and cook, covered, for 20 minutes, stirring occasionally.

Add the beans and cook for 5 minutes, or until the vegetables are cooked and the chicken is tender. Stir in the sugar, fish sauce and lime juice, adding extra sugar, fish sauce or lime juice to taste, if necessary.

Meanwhile, combine the rice and 250 ml (9 fl oz/1 cup) water in a small saucepan over a high heat. Bring to the boil and cover with a lid. Reduce the heat to medium–low and gently cook for 12–15 minutes or until all the water is absorbed.

Serve the chicken with the lime cheek and rice on the side.

Preparation time: 30 minutes   **Cooking time:** 30 minutes   **Serves:** 1 + 1

Preparation time: 10 minutes   **Cooking time:** 20 minutes   **Serves:** 1

Lamb steak with pecorino mash and artichokes

2 desiree potatoes, peeled and
  cut into chunks
2 tablespoons butter
2½ tablespoons milk
25 g (1 oz/¼ cup) finely grated
  pecorino cheese
1½ tablespoons olive oil
180 g (6 oz) lamb leg steak
125 ml (4 fl oz/½ cup) red wine
2 purchased artichoke hearts in oil,
  drained and quartered
½ garlic clove, crushed
1 teaspoon lemon juice
1 handful flat-leaf (Italian) parsley leaves

Cook the potatoes in boiling, salted water for about 10 minutes or until tender, then drain well. Return to the pan with half of the butter, the milk and the pecorino. Mash until smooth, then cover with a lid or foil to keep warm.

Meanwhile, place 2 teaspoons of the olive oil in a small heavy-based frying pan over high heat. When the oil is hot, add the steak and cook for 2–3 minutes on each side or until just cooked through. Remove the steak from the pan and set aside. Add the wine to the pan, stirring to remove any sediment from the base, then reduce the heat to low and gently boil for 2 minutes. Stir in the remaining butter and cook for 1–2 minutes, swirling the pan, until glossy. Season to taste with sea salt and freshly ground black pepper.

In a small bowl combine the artichoke, garlic, lemon juice, parsley and the remaining olive oil, and toss to combine well. Place the lamb on a serving plate with the mash and artichokes, and serve immediately with the sauce on the side.

Chilli, chicken and cashew stir-fry

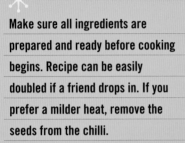

Make sure all ingredients are prepared and ready before cooking begins. Recipe can be easily doubled if a friend drops in. If you prefer a milder heat, remove the seeds from the chilli.

2 small chicken thigh fillets
(about 7 oz/200 g), sliced
1 teaspoon cornflour (cornstarch)
2 teaspoons soy sauce
2 teaspoons oyster sauce
½–1 red bird's eye chilli,
to taste, chopped
1 garlic clove, chopped
1 teaspoon grated fresh ginger
2 teaspoons vegetable or peanut oil
¼ red capsicum (pepper), trimmed,
seeded and thinly sliced
½ small (50 g) carrot, cut in half
lengthways, then thinly sliced
2 spring onions (scallions), trimmed well
and cut into 5 cm (2 inch) lengths
2 teaspoons Chinese rice wine, or sherry
1 tablespoon roasted cashew nuts
¼ teaspoon sesame oil (optional)
steamed rice, to serve

Combine the chicken, cornflour, soy sauce, oyster sauce, chilli, garlic and ginger in a small bowl, tossing to coat the chicken well. Cover and refrigerate for at least 30 minutes (chicken can be marinated up to 12 hours in advance).

Heat the oil in a wok or frying pan over a medium–high heat, then add the chicken mixture and stir-fry for 1 minute. Add the capsicum, carrot and spring onion and stir-fry for 1 minute or until the vegetables begin to soften and the chicken is browned. Add the rice wine, cashew nuts and sesame oil, if using, and toss to combine well. Remove from the heat and serve immediately with the steamed rice.

Preparation time: 15 minutes, plus at least 30 minutes marinating

Cooking time: 5 minutes

Serves: 1

Preparation time: 15 minutes   **Cooking time:** 30 minutes   **Serves:** 1

Poached beef with horseradish cream

160 g (5¾ oz) beef eye fillet, trimmed
500 ml (17 fl oz/2 cups) beef stock
4 black peppercorns
1 large French shallot, halved
½ bay leaf
1 thyme sprig
2 new potatoes, halved
3 baby carrots, peeled
2 asparagus spears, trimmed and halved
8 baby green beans, trimmed
1 tablespoon horseradish cream,
 or to taste

Using kitchen string, tie the fillet firmly around the middle to form a neat shape. Place the stock, peppercorns, shallot, bay leaf and thyme in a saucepan over medium heat and bring to the boil. Reduce heat to low and when gently boiling, add the potatoes and carrots and cook for 3–4 minutes, then add the beef and a little more stock or water to just cover, if necessary. Cook, uncovered, for about 6–10 minutes for medium, or until the steak is cooked to your liking and the vegetables are tender. (Cooking times will vary according to the thickness of the fillet. Remove the fillet earlier and continue cooking the vegetables until tender if necessary.) Remove the beef and set aside in a warm place.

Add the asparagus and beans to the stock and cook for about 3 minutes. Remove the vegetables when they are tender and keep warm with the fillet. Pour off half the stock, discarding the peppercorns, bay leaf and thyme, then boil the remaining mixture for about 10–15 minutes or until reduced to 60 ml (2 fl oz/¼ cup). Reheat the fillet and vegetables briefly in the reduced stock.

Place the fillet on a serving plate and remove the string. Place the vegetables around the steak, drizzle with remaining stock and serve immediately with the horseradish cream on the side.

Roast pork with honey and pomegranate carrots

½ teaspoon cumin seeds, crushed
½ teaspoon ground coriander
large pinch chilli flakes
2 teaspoons olive oil
150 g (5½ oz) pork tenderloin, trimmed
½ bunch baby carrots (about 6),
  trimmed and halved lengthways
1 teaspoon honey
½ teaspoon dijon mustard
1 tablespoon pomegranate molasses
1 handful coriander (cilantro) leaves
½ small red onion, thinly sliced
1 tablespoon Greek-style yoghurt

Preheat the oven to 200°C (400°F/Gas 6).

Combine the cumin seeds, coriander, chilli and 1 teaspoon of the olive oil in a bowl. Coat the pork with the mixture, then set aside.

Combine the carrots, honey and mustard in a small roasting tin, tossing to coat the carrot. Season to taste with sea salt and freshly ground black pepper, then roast for 15 minutes, turning the carrots occasionally. Remove the tin from the oven. Add the molasses to the carrots, tossing to coat, then add the pork, return the tin to the oven and cook for 10 minutes or until the pork is just cooked through. Remove the pork from the tin, cover loosely with foil and keep warm for 5 minutes.

Place the coriander leaves, onion and yoghurt in a bowl and gently toss to just combine.

To serve, place the carrots on a warmed plate, slice the pork into 3 or 4 pieces and place alongside the carrots. Add the coriander salad to the plate and serve immediately.

※ **Preparation time:** 15 minutes   ※ **Cooking time:** 25 minutes   ※ **Serves:** 1

Preparation time: 15 minutes, plus at least 20 minutes marinating

Cooking time: 10 minutes

Serves: 1

Yoghurt chicken with Indian spices

150 g (5½ oz) chicken breast fillet
1 teaspoon ground cumin
1 teaspoon freshly ground black pepper
½ teaspoon ground cinnamon
½ teaspoon turmeric
1 garlic clove, crushed
2 teaspoons grated fresh ginger
80 g (2¾ oz) Greek-style yoghurt
2 teaspoons olive oil
1 tomato, cut into wedges
⅓ cup mint
½ small red onion, thinly sliced
2 teaspoons lemon juice
sweet mango chutney and naan bread,
  to serve

Place the chicken fillet on a board. Using a large sharp knife and with one hand on top of the fillet to steady it, cut through the middle horizontally to butterfly the fillet; take care not to cut the fillet all the way through. Open the fillet up.

Heat a non-stick frying pan over a medium–high heat. Add the spices to the pan and cook, stirring, for 1 minute or until fragrant. Transfer the mixture to a bowl. Add the garlic, ginger and yoghurt to the spice mixture in the bowl, add the chicken and toss to coat in the mixture. Cover with plastic wrap, then refrigerate for at least 20 minutes and up to 8 hours.

Drain the chicken well. Place the oil in a frying pan over medium heat, add the chicken and cook for 4 minutes on each side, or until golden and cooked through. Season to taste with sea salt and freshly ground black pepper.

Combine the tomato, mint, onion and lemon juice in a small bowl. Place the chicken and tomato salad on a plate and serve with mango chutney and naan bread on the side.

Paprika fish with warm potato salad

1 potato, peeled and cut into
  2 cm (¾ inch) pieces
1 tablespoon mayonnaise
1 teaspoon light sour cream
½ teaspoon dijon mustard
1 spring onion (scallion), thinly sliced
1 teaspoon capers, chopped
1 garlic clove, crushed
1 tablespoon coriander (cilantro)
  leaves, chopped
1 teaspoon ground fennel seed
1 teaspoon ground paprika
½ teaspoon finely grated lemon rind
2 teaspoons plain (all-purpose) flour
200 g (7 oz) Nile Perch or basa fillets
1½ tablespoons extra virgin olive oil
1 teaspoon balsamic vinegar
1 small handful baby spinach leaves
lemon cheek, to serve

Cook the potato in boiling, salted water for about 8 minutes or until just tender, then drain well. Cool the potato.

Combine the mayonnaise, sour cream, mustard, spring onion, capers, garlic and coriander in a bowl. Add the potato and stir gently to combine well.

In a small bowl, combine the fennel, paprika, lemon rind and plain flour. Season to taste with sea salt and freshly ground black pepper. Dust the fish in the flour mixture, shaking off any excess. Heat 2 teaspoons of the oil in a small heatproof frying pan over medium heat, add the fish and cook for 2–3 minutes on each side, or until the fish is cooked through and golden brown.

Meanwhile, combine the balsamic vinegar and the remaining oil in a small jar or bowl and season to taste.

Place the fish, potato salad and spinach leaves on a serving plate with the lemon cheek. Serve immediately with the dressing on the side.

Preparation time: 10 minutes   Cooking time: 15 minutes   Serves: 1

Preparation time: 10 minutes, plus 20 minutes standing

Cooking time: 20 minutes

Serves: 1

Chinese poached chicken with bok choy

80 ml (2½ fl oz/⅓ cup) soy sauce
80 ml (2½ fl oz/⅓ cup) Chinese rice wine
45 g (1¾ oz/⅓ cup) grated palm
  sugar (jaggery)
½ star anise
2 garlic cloves, thinly sliced
2.5 cm (1 inch) strip orange zest,
  all white pith removed
2 cm (¾ inch) piece ginger,
  thinly sliced
2 chicken breast fillets, cut in
  half widthways
2½ teaspoons peanut oil
1 small red capsicum (pepper),
  halved lengthways, seeded and
  cut into 1 cm (½ inch) strips
120 g (4¼ oz, about 2) baby bok choys
  (pak choys), trimmed and cut in half
  lengthways through the root end
steamed rice, to serve

Combine the soy, rice wine, sugar, star anise, half the garlic, orange zest, ginger and 100 ml (3½ fl oz) water in a small saucepan, cover and bring slowly to the boil over medium–low heat. Reduce the heat to low and gently boil for 5 minutes. Add the chicken, then cover the pan and cook over very low heat for 5 minutes; the liquid should be barely boiling. Don't let the liquid come to a full boil or the chicken will be tough. Without removing the lid, remove the pan from the heat and stand for 20 minutes to allow the chicken to cook through and the flavours to develop.

Heat the oil in a wok over high heat, then add the capsicum and cook, tossing the wok, for 2 minutes or until slightly charred and softened. Add the bok choy and remaining garlic and cook, tossing often, for 1–2 minutes or until the bok choy begins to soften. Add 2½ tablespoons of the chicken cooking liquid to the wok and cook for 1 minute or until the liquid has reduced slightly and the vegetables are tender. Serve the chicken with the vegetables and steamed rice.

If two chicken fillets are too much, eat the second fillet the next day in a salad or sandwich. The chicken cooking liquid can be used again and again to poach chicken; after removing chicken, boil the stock for 5 minutes, strain and cool, then freeze in a ziplock bag. Simply thaw and bring back to the boil, topping it up with a little water as necessary. Each time you use it, it gains more flavour from the chicken that cooks in it.

Pork sausages with cabbage caraway braise

1 tablespoon butter
1 small onion, thinly sliced
1 potato, peeled and cut into
  2 cm (¾ inch) pieces
75 g (2¾ oz/1 cup) shredded cabbage
1 bay leaf
185 ml (6 fl oz/¾ cup) chicken stock
1 tablespoon red wine vinegar
1 teaspoon caraway seeds
2 teaspoons vegetable oil
2 thin pork sausages (about 200 g/
  7 oz each)
dijon mustard and flat-leaf (Italian)
  parsley, to serve

Apple sauce
1 granny smith apple
1 teaspoon lemon juice
2 teaspoons caster (superfine) sugar

Heat the butter in a saucepan over medium heat, add the onion and cook, stirring occasionally, for 5 minutes or until softened. Add the potato, cabbage, bay leaf, stock and vinegar, then season to taste with sea salt and freshly ground black pepper. Bring the mixture to the boil, cover, then reduce the heat to low and cook for about 25 minutes, or until the potatoes are tender and the liquid is absorbed. Remove the bay leaf and discard, then stir in the caraway seeds.

Meanwhile, to make the apple sauce, peel, core and thinly slice the apple. Place in a small saucepan with 2 tablespoons water, the lemon juice and caster sugar. Bring to the boil over medium heat, then reduce to low and cook for 20 minutes or until the apple is very soft. Stir to form a purée.

Heat the oil in a small heavy-based frying pan over medium–high heat. Add the sausages and cook, turning often, for 15 minutes or until golden and cooked through.

Place the cabbage and potato on a serving plate, place the sausages alongside and top with the apple sauce. Add a teaspoon of mustard, sprinkle with parsley leaves and serve immediately.

Preparation time: 15 minutes   Cooking time: 30 minutes   Serves: 1

Preparation time: 10 minutes, plus 10 minutes marinating

Cooking time: 5 minutes

Serves: 1

Five-spice lamb and sugarsnap stir-fry

1 garlic clove, crushed

¼ teaspoon five-spice powder

2 lamb fillets (about 150 g/5½ oz), trimmed and thinly sliced on the diagonal

50 g (1¾ oz) dried rice stick noodles

1 tablespoon hoisin sauce

2 teaspoons soy sauce

1 teaspoon grated fresh ginger

2 teaspoons peanut oil

1 spring onion (scallion), trimmed and sliced thickly on the diagonal

75 g (2¾ oz) oyster mushrooms, quartered

75 g (2¾ oz/¾ cup) sugarsnap peas, trimmed and strings removed

sliced red chilli, to serve

In a small bowl combine the garlic, five-spice powder and a large pinch of sea salt. Add the lamb and toss to coat well. Cover and stand for 10 minutes.

Place the noodles in a heatproof bowl. Pour over boiling water, cover and stand for 5–10 minutes or until tender. Drain and set aside to keep warm.

Combine the hoisin sauce, soy sauce, ginger and 1 tablespoon hot water in a small bowl. Place 1 teaspoon of the peanut oil in a wok over high heat, add the lamb and stir-fry for 1 minute or until just cooked through. Remove to a plate.

Add the remaining peanut oil to the wok, then add the spring onion, mushrooms and sugarsnap peas. Stir-fry for 2 minutes, then add the hoisin mixture and lamb. Cook, stirring, for 1 minute or until heated through. Place the rice noodles in a serving bowl, top with the lamb and serve sprinkled with the chilli slices.

This recipe would also work very well with chicken or raw prawns (shrimp) instead of the lamb.

Spatchcock with apricot couscous and zucchini

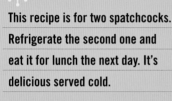

This recipe is for two spatchcocks. Refrigerate the second one and eat it for lunch the next day. It's delicious served cold.

2 tablespoons olive oil
45 g (1¾ oz/¼ cup) couscous
2 tablespoons chopped dried apricots
2 tablespoons chopped toasted
   slivered almonds
2½ tablespoons chopped flat-leaf
   (Italian) parsley
2½ tablespoons chopped mint
2 tablespoons lemon juice
2 teaspoons finely grated lemon rind
2 x 450 g (1 lb) spatchcocks
2 teaspoons butter
1 small zucchini (courgette), ends
   trimmed and thickly sliced
50 ml (1½ fl oz) white wine

Preheat the oven to 190°C (375°F/Gas 5). Spread half the olive oil over the base of a small roasting tin.

Combine the couscous, apricots, almonds, 2 tablespoons of the parsley, 2 tablespoons of the mint, 2 teaspoons of the oil, and the lemon juice and rind in a bowl. Pour over 60 ml (2 fl oz/¼ cup) hot water, cover and stand for 10 minutes or until the water is absorbed. Season to taste with sea salt and freshly ground black pepper.

Rinse the spatchcocks under running water and pat inside and out with paper towels. Spoon the couscous mixture into the cavities, using the back of a spoon to push it in firmly. Fold the wings under the body. Cross the legs together and tie firmly with kitchen string.

Rub the skin with the remaining oil, then transfer the spatchcocks, breast side up, to the roasting tin and roast for 45 minutes or until the juices run clear when tested with a skewer inserted into the thigh and the couscous is hot when tested with a skewer inserted into the centre of the cavity. Set aside for 5 minutes.

Heat the butter in a frying pan over medium heat, add the zucchini and cook, shaking the pan often, for 3–4 minutes or until tender. Add the wine and remaining herbs, season to taste, then transfer to a serving plate.

Place the stuffed spatchcock on the plate alongside the zucchini, pour over the roasting juices and serve immediately.

✳ **Preparation time:** 20 minutes, plus 10 minutes standing   ✳ **Cooking time:** 50 minutes   ✳ **Serves:** 1 + 1

✳ Preparation time: 30 minutes   **✳ Cooking time:** 50 minutes   **✳ Serves:** 1 + 1

Individual seafood and tarragon pies

60 g (2¼ oz) butter

1 small garlic clove, crushed

2 French shallots, quartered

100 g (3½ oz) Swiss brown
  mushrooms, sliced

5 raw king prawns (shrimp), peeled,
  cleaned and halved lengthways

100 g (3½ oz) scallops, cleaned
  and halved

200 g (7 oz) firm, white-fleshed fish
  fillet, such as ling or dory, cut into
  2 cm (¾ inch) pieces

2 teaspoons finely chopped tarragon

1 tablespoon plain (all-purpose) flour

1 teaspoon dry mustard powder

60 ml (2 fl oz/¼ cup) white wine

200 ml (7 fl oz) cream

60 g (2¼ oz/½ cup) grated
  cheddar cheese

Potato topping

3 potatoes, such as King Edward
  or other good mashing potatoes,
  peeled and chopped

1 tablespoon butter

60 ml (2 fl oz/¼ cup) milk

1½ tablespoons finely chopped chives

To make the potato topping, cook the potato in boiling, salted water for 15–20 minutes or until tender. Drain well, then return to the saucepan over very low heat. Add the butter and milk and season to taste with sea salt and freshly ground black pepper. Using a potato masher, mash until the potatoes are smooth, then add the chives and mix through. Remove from the heat, cover the pan and keep warm.

Preheat the oven to 180°C (350°F/Gas 4).

Heat 2 tablespoons of the butter in a small frying pan over medium–low heat, then add the garlic, shallots and mushrooms. Cook, stirring often, for 5 minutes or until the mushrooms are soft. Add the prawns, scallops and fish, and cook for 3 minutes, turning occasionally. Transfer to a small bowl and stir in the tarragon.

Place the remaining butter in a small saucepan, add the flour and mustard and stir until a paste forms. Stirring constantly, add the wine and cream. Stir until the mixture comes to a gentle boil, taking care that no lumps form, then cook, stirring, for 3–4 minutes or until the mixture is thick and smooth. Add the seafood mixture and cheese, stir to combine well, then cook over a low heat for 2–3 minutes to heat through.

Divide the mixture between two 500 ml (17 fl oz/2 cup) capacity ovenproof ramekins (dariole moulds), or individual pie dishes. Place a heaped spoon of potato mash over the seafood mixture, spreading to cover evenly (see tip). Place 1 pie on a baking tray and bake for 15–20 minutes or until golden and bubbling Serve immediately.

Freeze the second pie for later use. Wrap the unbaked pie in plastic wrap, then wrap in foil and place in an airtight freezer bag. Refrigerate until chilled, then freeze. Label and date as it's best eaten within 1 month of freezing. To reheat, defrost in the fridge for 24 hours, remove the foil and plastic wrap and bake as described in the method.

Red flannel hash

This is a great recipe for using left-over cooked potato. This recipe makes four hash patties. Extra patties will keep refrigerated for 3–4 days. Reheat in a frying pan and try them for breakfast.

250 g (9 oz) potatoes, such as dutch cream or other good mashing potato (about 2 small), scrubbed
100 g (3½ oz) tinned whole baby beetroot (beets), drained
100 g (3½ oz) cooked corned beef, cut into 1 cm (½ inch) pieces
1 small onion, very finely chopped
2 tablespoons chopped flat-leaf (Italian) parsley, plus a few extra leaves, to serve
2 teaspoons wholegrain mustard
60 ml (2 fl oz/¼ cup) olive oil
1 egg
ready-made tomato chutney, to serve

Place the potato in a saucepan, cover with cold water and bring to the boil over medium heat. Cook for 20 minutes or until tender, then drain well, season with sea salt and coarsely mash.

Cut the beetroot into 1 cm (½ inch) pieces, then combine with the corned beef, onion, parsley, mustard and potato in a bowl. Season to taste with sea salt and freshly ground black pepper.

Brush the inside edge of 4 egg-poaching rings with some of the oil. Heat 2 tablespoons of the oil in a non-stick frying pan over medium heat. Place the rings in the pan. Spoon the potato mixture into the rings and use the back of a spoon to flatten it into the rings. Cook for 6–7 minutes or until browned and crisp on the bottom. Turn over and cook for a further 3–5 minutes or until golden brown.

Heat the remaining oil in a small non-stick frying pan over a medium heat. Break in the egg and cook for 3 minutes or until just set. Place 2 flannel hash patties on a serving plate, top with the parsley leaves and remove the egg rings. Add the fried egg and serve immediately with the tomato chutney.

Preparation time: 15 minutes   **Cooking time:** 35 minutes   **Serves:** 1 + 1

Preparation time: 5 minutes   **Cooking time:** 10 minutes   **Serves:** 1

Minute steak with brandy cream

1 minute steak (about 150 g/5½ oz)
2 tablespoons butter
1 garlic clove, crushed
2 tablespoons brandy
1 teaspoon dijon mustard
50 ml (1½ fl oz) cream
2 teaspoons lemon juice
½ baby cos (romaine) lettuce,
  cut in wedges
lemon wedges and sliced baguette,
  to serve

Season the steak well on both sides with sea salt and freshly ground black pepper. Melt the butter in a heavy-based frying pan over medium–high heat. Cook the steak for 1 minute on each side or until browned. Remove from the pan and set aside.

Reduce the heat to medium–low. Add the garlic to the pan and cook for 30 seconds. Add the brandy and bring to the boil. Cook, stirring, for 1 minute or until half the liquid has evaporated. Reduce the heat to low. Add the mustard and cream and cook, stirring, for 1–2 minutes or until the sauce has thickened slightly. Remove from the heat and season to taste.

Pour the lemon juice over the lettuce and place on a serving plate. Place the steak alongside the lettuce and top with the brandy sauce. Serve immediately with the lemon wedges and bread on the side.

Chicken ravioli with lemon burnt butter

Ravioli can be made up to 3 hours in advance; cover and refrigerate until ready to cook. You could easily double this recipe to make extra ravioli and freeze them for another day. Freeze in a single layer in an airtight plastic bag. When ready to use, cook over medium heat for 8–10 minutes.

100 g (3½ oz) minced (ground) chicken
1 tablespoon currants
1 tablespoon toasted pine nuts,
  plus extra, to serve
2–3 anchovy fillets, finely chopped
1 tablespoon finely chopped parsley
1 teaspoon finely chopped rosemary
1 teaspoon finely chopped oregano,
  plus a few leaves extra, to serve
8 won ton wrappers

Lemon burnt butter
15 g (½ oz) butter
¼ lemon, zested
1–2 teaspoons lemon juice

Combine the chicken mince, currants, pine nuts, anchovies and herbs in a bowl and season to taste with sea salt and freshly ground black pepper. Stir to mix well. Lay half the won ton wrappers on a baking paper-lined baking tray, then place about 1 tablespoon of the filling onto the centre of each wrapper, flattening slightly. Using a brush, lightly brush the edges of each wrapper with water to dampen slightly, then place the remaining wrappers on top of each, pressing down the edges lightly to seal.

To make the lemon burnt butter, melt the butter in a small saucepan over medium–low heat, then cook for about 1 minute or until the butter and its solids begin to turn golden brown. Remove from the heat and add the lemon zest and juice.

Bring a large saucepan of water to the boil, add the ravioli and cook for 5 minutes or until cooked through. Drain well. To serve, place the ravioli onto a serving plate, drizzle with the lemon burnt butter, sprinkle with the extra pine nuts and oregano leaves, and serve immediately.

Preparation time: 25 minutes   **Cooking time:** 10 minutes   **Serves:** 1

Desserts

Peanut brittle ice cream with chocolate sauce • Lemon-rosemary baked custard • Grilled figs with honeyed mascarpone • Strawberries with ricotta cream and mint • Individual apple-blueberry pie • Brandy-caramel pear • Banana in lemongrass syrup with coconut cream • Baked apple with marzipan • Raspberry syllabub • Cardamom-poached pear with ginger-biscuit cream • Hazelnut and blackberry clafoutis • Cherry-brioche trifle • Earl Grey and ginger-steeped dates • Passionfruit yoghurt ice cream with fruit • Torrijas with honey cream • Espresso jelly • Pineapple and lime millefeuille • Prune and pistachio 'sandwiches' • Plum and sour cream gratin • Caramel cream

Peanut brittle ice cream with chocolate sauce

300 g (10½ oz) chocolate ice cream
50 g (1¾ oz) peanut brittle, chopped
30 g (1 oz) chopped dark chocolate
2 tablespoons cream

Place the ice cream in a small bowl for 5 minutes or until just softened, then add the peanut brittle and stir to combine well. Place the ice cream in a small freezer-proof container, cover and freeze for at least 2 hours.

Combine the chocolate and cream in a small saucepan and place over very low heat for 2–3 minutes, stirring occasionally, until the chocolate has melted and the sauce is smooth.

To serve, scoop the ice cream into a bowl, pour over the sauce and serve immediately.

You can easily change the peanut brittle to your favourite treat such as Turkish delight or chocolate-covered honeycomb.

Lemon-rosemary baked custard

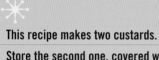

This recipe makes two custards. Store the second one, covered with plastic wrap, in the refrigerator for 2–3 days. Try it served chilled.

250 ml (9 fl oz/1 cup) milk
125 ml (4 fl oz/½ cup) cream
55 g (2 oz/½ cup) caster
  (superfine) sugar
2 teaspoons finely chopped rosemary
2 teaspoons finely chopped lemon zest
2 eggs, plus 1 egg yolk

Rosemary and pine-nut toffee shards
butter, for greasing
80 g (2¾ oz) caster (superfine) sugar
1 tablespoon chopped pine nuts
½ teaspoon very finely chopped rosemary

To make the rosemary and pine-nut toffee shards, grease a sheet of foil and place on a baking tray. Place the sugar and 2 tablespoons water in a small saucepan over medium–low heat and bring to the boil, stirring constantly. Reduce the heat to low and gently boil until the syrup is pale golden. Quickly swirl in the nuts and rosemary and immediately pour onto the prepared tray. Leave to cool and set.

Preheat the oven to 150°C (300°F/Gas 2). Grease two 300 ml (10½ fl oz) capacity ovenproof ramekins (dariole moulds) or teacups.

Combine the milk, cream, sugar, rosemary and lemon zest in a small saucepan over medium–low heat and, stirring occasionally, bring mixture almost to the boil. Remove from the heat and stand for 10 minutes for the mixture to infuse.

Place the eggs and yolk in a bowl and whisk to combine. Pour the warm milk mixture through a fine strainer onto the eggs, discarding solids, then whisk until just combined. Pour into the prepared ramekins. Place the ramekins in a baking dish and add enough boiling water to come halfway up the sides of the ramekins. Bake for 40 minutes, or until the custard is just set in the middle. It should still be slightly wobbly; to test, insert a knife in the centre of the custard and if it comes out clean, the custard is ready.

Break the toffee into shards and sprinkle over the custard. Serve warm or at room temperature.

Grilled figs with honeyed mascarpone

55 g (2 oz/¼ cup) mascarpone cheese
1 teaspoon honey
2 figs, cut in half lengthways
1 tablespoon firmly packed brown sugar
2 teaspoons toasted flaked almonds

Preheat the grill (broiler) to medium.

Combine the mascarpone and honey in a serving bowl.

Place the figs, skin side down, on a small baking tray, sprinkle with the sugar and grill for 3 minutes or until the sugar is melted and the figs are golden. Transfer to a serving bowl, sprinkle with the almonds and serve immediately with the mascarpone mixture.

When figs are not in season, try grilled plums, nectarines or even pineapple or pear.

Strawberries with ricotta cream and mint

125 g (4½ oz) strawberries, hulled
  and halved
2 teaspoons Cointreau
  (orange-flavoured liqueur)
1½ tablespoons icing (confectioner's)
  sugar, sifted
80 g (2¾ oz/⅓ cup) ricotta cheese
1 tablespoon thick (double/heavy) cream
1 tablespoon small mint leaves
1 teaspoon toasted pistachio kernels,
  roughly chopped

Combine the strawberries, Cointreau and half the icing sugar in a small bowl. Toss well to combine, then stand at room temperature for 30 minutes or until the strawberries soften slightly.

Meanwhile combine the remaining icing sugar, ricotta and cream in a small bowl. Toss the strawberries with the mint leaves and transfer to a glass, sprinkle with the pistachios and serve immediately with the ricotta cream on the side.

Preparation time: 10 minutes, plus 30 minutes standing

Cooking time: nil

Serves: 1

Preparation time: 15 minutes   **Cooking time:** 40 minutes   **Serves:** 1

Individual apple-blueberry pie

butter, for greasing
1 sheet frozen shortcrust pastry,
  partially thawed
2 tablespoons plain (all-purpose) flour
2 tablespoons brown sugar
1 tablespoon unsalted butter, softened
2 tablespoons coarsely chopped
  walnut pieces
80 g (2¾ oz/¼ cup) apple purée
1 tablespoon fresh or frozen blueberries
icing (confectioner's) sugar, to serve

Preheat the oven to 220°C (425°F/Gas 7).

Grease the base and side of an 8 cm (3¼ inch) loose-based flan (tart) tin. Cut the pastry in half diagonally, then use one piece to line the tin, easing it in to fit and trimming the edges. Line the pastry with baking paper, then fill with baking beads or dried beans. Place on a baking tray and bake for 20 minutes. Remove from the oven and remove the paper and baking beads.

Meanwhile, combine the flour and sugar in a bowl. Using your hands, rub the butter into the mixture to combine. Stir in the walnuts. Spoon the apple purée into the pastry case, sprinkle over the berries, then the walnut mixture. Bake for 20 minutes or until the topping has browned lightly. Cool slightly, then serve dusted with the icing sugar.

Brandy-caramel pear

2 tablespoons caster (superfine) sugar
1 tablespoon cream
1 tablespoon brandy
small pinch ground cinnamon
1 ripe beurre bosc pear, peeled,
  quartered and cored
vanilla ice cream, to serve

Combine the sugar and 1 tablespoon water in a small frying pan over medium heat. Cook for 4–5 minutes, shaking the pan occasionally, until the sugar has dissolved and is light golden. Do not stir. When the sugar is dark golden, remove from the heat and add the cream, taking care as the mixture will spit, then stir until the mixture is smooth. Add the brandy, cinnamon and pears. Return to a low heat and cook for 2 minutes or until the pears are heated through and coated in the brandy-caramel sauce. Spoon into a serving bowl and serve with a scoop of ice cream.

Preparation time: 10 minutes   **Cooking time:** 10 minutes   **Serves:** 1

✳ **Preparation time:** 10 minutes   ✳ **Cooking time:** 5 minutes   ✳ **Serves:** 1

Banana in lemongrass syrup with coconut cream

2 tablespoons caster (superfine) sugar
2 teaspoons thinly sliced lemongrass
2 teaspoons lime juice, or to taste
¼ teaspoon finely grated lime rind
1 firm banana
1½ tablespoons coconut cream, to serve
1 tablespoon shredded coconut,
  toasted (optional)

Combine the sugar and 80 ml (2½ fl oz/⅓ cup) water in a small saucepan and bring slowly to a gentle boil. Cook over medium heat for 3–4 minutes or until reduced and syrupy, then remove from the heat and cool. Stir in the lemongrass, lime juice and rind. Cut the banana into thin slices and place in a serving glass or bowl. Pour over the syrup, then top with the coconut cream and sprinkle with the shredded coconut, if using. Serve immediately.

Baked apple with marzipan

To ensure the apples sit flat in the dish, cut a very thin slice from the base of each apple. The extra apple will keep refrigerated for 3–4 days. To serve, reheat in a 190°C (375°F/Gas 5) oven for 10–15 minutes.

butter, for greasing
2 granny smith apples
40 g (1½ oz) marzipan, finely chopped
1 tablespoon finely chopped mixed peel
1 tablespoon finely chopped
  dark chocolate
1 tablespoon slivered almonds
1 tablespoon unsalted butter
1½ tablespoons honey
1½ tablespoons amaretto or brandy
thick vanilla custard or whipped cream,
  to serve

Preheat the oven to 190°C (375°F/Gas 5). Grease a deep 1 litre (35 fl oz /4 cup) capacity ovenproof dish.

Peel the top one-third of each apple, then, using an apple corer, remove the cores. Place the apples in the prepared dish.

Combine the marzipan and mixed peel and place a quarter of the mixture in each apple cavity, pressing it in firmly. Spoon the chocolate into each apple, pressing it in firmly, then top with the remaining marzipan mixture, pressing to mound the mixture on the top of each apple. Press in the almonds.

In a small saucepan, combine the butter, 2 tablespoons water, honey and amaretto or brandy and stir over a low heat until boiling. Spoon the mixture over the apples.

Cover the dish with foil, then bake for 30 minutes. Remove the foil and bake for another 15 minutes or until the apples are tender and the topping is golden. Cool slightly, then place an apple in a serving bowl, spoon the sauce over and serve with the custard or whipped cream.

Preparation time: 15 minutes   **Cooking time:** 50 minutes   **Serves:** 1 + 1

Raspberry syllabub

125 ml (4 fl oz/½ cup) thick
  (double/heavy) cream
1 teaspoon Crème de Cassis
  (blackcurrant-flavoured liqueur)
1 tablespoon caster (superfine) sugar
90 g (3¼ oz/¾ cup) fresh or thawed
  frozen raspberries, plus extra, to serve
purchased almond bread, to serve

Combine the cream, Crème de Cassis and half
the caster sugar in a bowl. Using electric
beaters, whisk the mixture until soft peaks form.

Combine the remaining sugar and the
raspberries in a bowl and mash to a coarse purée
with a fork. Gently stir the mashed raspberries
into the cream mixture, then divide among two
250 ml (9 fl oz/1 cup) capacity glasses. Cover
and refrigerate for 1–2 hours. Top with the extra
raspberries and serve immediately, with almond
bread on the side.

This recipe makes two desserts.
Store the second one, covered
with plastic wrap, in the refrigerator.
It's best eaten the next day.

Cardamom-poached pear with ginger-biscuit cream

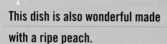

This dish is also wonderful made with a ripe peach.

55 g (2 oz/¼ cup) caster (superfine) sugar
½ cinnamon stick
2 cardamom pods, lightly crushed
1 teaspoon rosewater
1 firm beurre bosc pear
100 ml (3½ fl oz) cream
¼ teaspoon natural vanilla extract
1 purchased gingernut or other hard, ginger-flavoured biscuit, crushed

Combine the sugar, 250 ml (9 fl oz/1 cup) water, cinnamon, cardamom and rosewater in a small saucepan over medium heat and bring to the boil. Lower the pear into the syrup, reduce the heat to low and cook for 5 minutes. Take the pan off the heat and stand until cooled. When cool enough to handle, remove the pear and peel.

Return the syrup to a medium–low heat, bring to the boil, then cook for 3–5 minutes or until thickened and syrupy.

Combine the cream and vanilla in a small bowl and lightly whip until soft peaks form. Fold through the crushed biscuit.

Place the ginger-biscuit cream in a shallow bowl, place the pear on top and serve with the syrup on the side.

✳ **Preparation time:** 10 minutes   ✳ **Cooking time:** 15 minutes   ✳ **Serves:** 1

Preparation time: 10 minutes   **Cooking time:** 15 minutes   **Serves:** 1

Hazelnut and blackberry clafoutis

butter, for greasing
10 frozen or fresh blackberries
1 egg, lightly beaten
2 teaspoons Frangelico
  (hazelnut-flavoured liqueur)
1 tablespoon caster (superfine) sugar
1 tablespoon plain (all-purpose) flour
100 ml (3½ fl oz) cream, plus
  extra, to serve
1 tablespoon roasted hazelnuts, skin
  removed and roughly chopped
icing (confectioner's) sugar, to dust

Preheat the oven to 200°C (400°F/Gas 6).

Lightly grease a 250 ml (9 fl oz/1 cup) capacity shallow soufflé dish or ovenproof ceramic ramekin (dariole mould) with melted butter. Place the blackberries in the dish.

Whisk together the egg, Frangelico, sugar and flour. Add the cream and mix until the mixture is smooth. Pour over the blackberries and sprinkle with the hazelnuts. Bake for 10–15 minutes or until just firm to the touch and risen. Dust with the icing sugar and serve with a drizzle of cream.

Cherry-brioche trifle

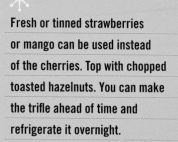

Fresh or tinned strawberries or mango can be used instead of the cherries. Top with chopped toasted hazelnuts. You can make the trifle ahead of time and refrigerate it overnight.

180 g (6 oz/⅔ cup) tinned pitted morello cherries in syrup
2 teaspoons caster (superfine) sugar
1½ tablespoons brandy or Cointreau (orange-flavoured liqueur)
½ cinnamon stick
1 teaspoon lemon juice
30 g (1 oz/½ cup) brioche, cut into 2 cm (¾ inch) cubes
80 ml (2½ fl oz/⅓ cup) vanilla custard
2 tablespoons thick (double/heavy) cream
1 tablespoon toasted flaked almonds

Combine the cherries and their syrup, sugar, brandy or Cointreau, cinnamon and lemon juice in a small saucepan over medium heat. Bring to the boil, then reduce the heat to low and cook gently for 4–5 minutes or until the liquid is reduced and thickened slightly. Remove from the heat, remove the cinnamon stick, then cool to room temperature.

Arrange half the brioche pieces in a 500 ml (17 fl oz/2 cup) capacity dessert glass. Spoon over half the warm cherries and juice. Pour over half the custard. Repeat with the remaining brioche, cherries and custard. Cover and refrigerate for at least 1 hour or until chilled.

Serve topped with the cream and sprinkled with the almonds.

Preparation time: 10 minutes, plus at least 1 hour chilling

Cooking time: 5 minutes

Serves: 1

✷ **Preparation time:** 5 minutes, plus overnight refrigeration

✷ **Cooking time:** nil

✷ **Serves:** 1

Earl Grey and ginger-steeped dates

4 fresh dates
1 Earl Grey teabag
10 cm (4 inch) strip orange zest
2 cm (¾ inch) piece ginger, sliced
1 tablespoon brown sugar
2 scoops vanilla ice cream, to serve

Using a small, sharp knife, make a neat cut in the side of each date and remove the stones. Combine the dates, teabag, orange zest, ginger and sugar in a small heatproof bowl, pour over 185 ml (6 fl oz/¾ cup) boiling water, then cool to room temperature. Cover and refrigerate overnight. Discard the teabag, ginger and orange zest.

Spoon the dates and a small amount of juice into a bowl and serve with a couple of scoops of vanilla ice cream.

Tea-steeped dates will keep refrigerated in an airtight container for up to 7 days.

Passionfruit yoghurt ice cream with fruit

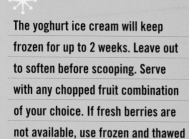

The yoghurt ice cream will keep frozen for up to 2 weeks. Leave out to soften before scooping. Serve with any chopped fruit combination of your choice. If fresh berries are not available, use frozen and thawed berries, sweetened to taste. Use tinned chopped fruit if fresh is not available.

500 g (1 lb 2 oz/2 cups) Greek-style yoghurt
125 g (4½ oz/1 cup) icing (confectioner's) sugar
125 ml (4 fl oz/½ cup) cream
170 g (5¾ oz) tin passionfruit pulp in syrup
125 g (4½ oz/½ cup) mixed berries and chopped fruit, such as kiwi fruit and banana

Combine the yoghurt, icing sugar and cream in a small, freezer-proof container. Add the passionfruit and stir to mix well. Cover the mixture tightly, then freeze for 1 hour or until well chilled. Transfer to an ice-cream machine, churn according to the manufacturer's instructions, then freeze until firm. If you do not have an ice-cream machine, after the 1 hour chilling, beat the yoghurt with electric beaters to break up the ice crystals, then re-freeze for 1 hour. Beat and freeze three more times; then cover and freeze until firm.

Soften the yoghurt ice cream at room temperature for about 10 minutes before serving. Place 2 scoops in a serving bowl or glass, add the chopped fruit and serve.

Preparation time: 10 minutes, plus churning/freezing

Cooking time: nil

Serves: 1 + 1

☀ **Preparation time:** 10 minutes   ☀ **Cooking time:** 5 minutes   ☀ **Serves:** 1

Torrijas with honey cream

125 ml (4 fl oz/½ cup) milk
1 tablespoon honey
¼ teaspoon ground ginger
¼ teaspoon natural vanilla extract
2 x 1.5 cm (⅝ inch) thick slices of stale
  baguette, sliced on an angle
2 tablespoons vegetable oil
30 g (1 oz/¼ cup) raspberries or other
  berries, to serve
1 teaspoon ground cinnamon
1 teaspoon caster (superfine) sugar

Honey cream

2 teaspoons honey
2 tablespoons thick (double/heavy) cream

To make the honey cream, combine the honey and cream in a bowl and mix well, then cover and refrigerate until needed.

Combine the milk, honey, ginger and vanilla in a small saucepan and stir over low heat until the honey is dissolved. Pour into a shallow bowl. Dip the bread slices into the milk mixture, allowing each slice to become quite soaked.

Heat the oil in a large non-stick frying pan over medium heat. Cook the bread slices for 2 minutes on each side or until golden. Place on a serving plate, top with the raspberries, sprinkle with the combined cinnamon and sugar and drizzle with the honey cream. Serve immediately.

Espresso jelly

1½ tablespoons strong espresso coffee
1 tablespoon caster (superfine) sugar,
   or to taste
1 teaspoon powdered gelatine
thick (double/heavy) cream,
   shaved dark chocolate
   and coffee liqueur, to serve

Add boiling water to the espresso to make up to 125 ml (4 fl oz/½ cup), then stir the sugar into the coffee to taste. Sprinkle over the gelatine and stir to dissolve.

Pour into a 185 ml (6 fl oz/¾ cup) capacity serving glass, then cool to room temperature. Cover with plastic wrap and refrigerate for 2–3 hours or until set.

To serve, spoon over the thick cream to taste, then sprinkle with some shaved chocolate. Drizzle with a little coffee liqueur and serve.

Preparation time: 5 minutes, plus at least 2 hours chilling

Cooking time: nil

Serves: 1

Pineapple and lime millefeuille

80 ml (2½ fl oz/⅓ cup) thick
    (double/heavy) cream
½ teaspoon finely grated lime rind
2½ teaspoons finely grated palm
    sugar (jaggery)
¼ sheet frozen puff pastry, thawed
100 g (3½ oz) 5 mm (¼ inch) thick
    slice pineapple, trimmed, cored and
    cut into 1 cm (½ inch) pieces
icing (confectioner's) sugar, to serve

Preheat the oven to 200°C (400°F/Gas 6). Line a baking tray with baking paper.

Place the cream, lime rind and 1½ teaspoons of the palm sugar in a small bowl and whisk until firm peaks form. Cover and refrigerate until needed.

Cut the square of pastry in half so you have two 5 x 12 cm (2 x 4½ inch) rectangles. Place the pastry at one end of the baking tray and place the pineapple, in a single layer, at the other end. Sprinkle the pineapple with the remaining palm sugar. Cook for 8–10 minutes or until the pastry is puffed and golden and the pineapple has softened. Cool the pastry and pineapple to room temperature. Using a sharp, serrated knife, cut the pastry rectangles open, so you have a top and a bottom piece. Place 1 bottom piece on a serving plate. Spoon a third of the cream over, then top with a third of the pineapple. Repeat with the remaining pastry, cream and pineapple, finishing with a piece of pastry. Dust with the icing sugar and serve immediately.

Prune and pistachio 'sandwiches'

Any left-over prune mixture will keep well in an airtight container in the refrigerator. You could use sherry or port instead of the red wine, if you like.

140 g (5 oz/⅔ cup) whole pitted prunes
80 ml (2½ fl oz/⅓ cup) orange juice
80 ml (2½ fl oz/⅓ cup) red wine
1 tablespoon firmly packed brown sugar
¼ teaspoon ground cinnamon
pinch ground cloves
½ teaspoon finely grated orange rind
2 tablespoons chopped pistachios
2 oat biscuits
icing (confectioner's) sugar and vanilla
   ice cream, to serve

Combine the prunes, orange juice and wine in a small bowl, cover with plastic wrap, then stand at room temperature for at least 2 hours or overnight. Combine the prune mixture, sugar, cinnamon, cloves and orange rind in a small saucepan over medium–low heat, cover, then bring to a gentle boil. Cook for 4–5 minutes or until the prunes are tender. Cool the prunes, then strain, reserving the liquid.

When the prunes are cool, mash with a fork to form a coarse purée, then stir in the pistachios. Spread 1 oat biscuit with half the prune mixture, then top with another biscuit. Dust with the icing sugar. If you like, drizzle with the reserved poaching liquid, then serve with a scoop of ice cream.

Preparation time: 20 minutes, plus at least 2 hours standing

Cooking time: 5 minutes

Serves: 1

Preparation time: 15 minutes, plus 30 minutes chilling

Cooking time: 2 minutes

Serves: 1

Plum and sour cream gratin

3 plums, halved and stones removed
1½ tablespoons caster (superfine) sugar
2 teaspoons finely chopped glacé ginger
60 g (2¼ oz/¼ cup) sour cream
1 tablespoon chopped toasted pistachios

Place the plum halves, cut side up, in a
250 ml (9 fl oz/ 1 cup) capacity ovenproof dish.
Combine 2 teaspoons of the sugar with the
ginger and sour cream and drizzle over the
plums. Refrigerate for 30 minutes.

Preheat the grill (broiler) to very high. Place
the dish on a baking tray, sprinkle over the
remaining sugar and place as close to the heat
as possible for 1–2 minutes until the sugar
caramelises. Cool slightly, then serve immediately
with the pistachios sprinkled over the top.

If fresh plums are not in season,
use 3 whole tinned plums instead,
drained and halved.

Caramel cream

185 ml (6 fl oz/¾ cup) cream
75 g (2¾ oz) purchased soft,
  chewy caramel sweets (about 8),
  roughly chopped
1 tablespoon flaked almonds,
  lightly toasted

Place 60 ml (2 fl oz/¼ cup) of the cream and the caramel sweets in a small saucepan over low heat. Cook, stirring constantly, for 3–5 minutes or until the caramels have dissolved and the mixture is smooth. Remove from the heat and cool to room temperature.

Whisk the remaining cream until soft peaks form, then gently fold through the cooled caramel mixture. Spoon into a serving dish or glass, sprinkle with the almonds and serve.

Preparation time: 10 minutes   **Cooking time:** 5 minutes   **Serves:** 1

INDEX

A

apple

apple, baked, with marzipan   162

apple–blueberry pie, individual   157

artichokes

lamb steak with pecorino mash and artichokes   119

poached chicken and artichoke salad with
saffron aïoli   96

asparagus and tofu salad with sesame dressing   61

B

banana in lemongrass syrup with coconut cream   161

BBQ duck and hoisin wrap   66

beans

garlicky white bean brandade   45

golden haloumi with bean and olive salad   18

beef

beef and cashew noodle salad   42

easy beef fajitas   111

fillet steak with blue cheese butter and
cauliflower crush   112

Italian-style beef with vegetables   88

minute steak with brandy cream   143

poached beef with horseradish cream   123

red flannel hash   140

sesame beef salad with avocado and grapefruit   22

Vietnamese lemongrass beef stir-fry   84

brandade, garlicky white bean   45

brandy–caramel pear   158

burger, lamb, with hummus and beetroot   58

C

capsicum, spicy capsicum and tomato bake with egg   49

caramel

brandy–caramel pear   158

caramel cream   186

caramel tofu with peanuts and ginger   69

cardamom-poached pear with ginger-biscuit cream   166

cheese

croque monsieur, pastrami and fontina   70

golden haloumi with bean and olive salad   18

grilled figs with honeyed mascarpone   153

pork, brie and apricot sandwich   37

individual fondue   54

soft cheese and walnut polenta with mushrooms   21

soufflé omelette with ham and gruyère cheese   33

strawberries with ricotta cream and mint   154

tortellini stracciatella   34

warm eggplant and feta salad   30

cherry-brioche trifle   170

chicken

chargrilled piri-piri spatchcock   83

chicken, corn and noodle soup   25

chicken ravioli with lemon burnt butter   144

chilli, chicken and cashew stir-fry   120

Chinese poached chicken with bok choy   131

Malay-style chicken curry   116

poached chicken and artichoke salad with
saffron aïoli   96

quick chicken and mushroom pie   92

smoked chicken Waldorf salad on bruschetta   62

spatchcock with apricot couscous and zucchini   136

spiced chicken quesadillas   41

yoghurt chicken with Indian spices   127

chilli, chicken and cashew stir-fry   120

Chinese poached chicken with bok choy   131

Chinese roast pork with orange sauce   99

clafoutis, hazelnut and blackberry   169

crisp-skin blue eye trevalla with potatoes
and red coleslaw   79

croque monsieur, pastrami and fontina   70

curry, Malay-style chicken   116

custard, lemon–rosemary baked   150

D

dates, Earl Grey and ginger-steeped   173

desserts

baked apple with marzipan   162

banana in lemongrass syrup with coconut cream   161

brandy–caramel pear   158

caramel cream   186

cardamom-poached pear with ginger-biscuit cream   166

cherry-brioche trifle   170

Earl Grey and ginger-steeped dates   173

espresso jelly	178
grilled figs with honeyed mascarpone	153
hazelnut and blackberry clafoutis	169
individual apple–blueberry pie	157
lemon–rosemary baked custard	150
passionfruit yoghurt ice cream with fruit	174
peanut brittle ice cream with chocolate sauce	149
pineapple and lime millefeuille	181
plum and sour cream gratin	185
prune and pistachio 'sandwiches'	182
raspberry syllabub with almond bread	165
strawberries with ricotta cream and mint	154
torrijas with honey cream	177

dressings

apple sauce	132
blue cheese butter	112
chardonnay sauce	104
chilli dressing	13
ginger dressing	22
lemon and honey	18
sesame dressing	61
yoghurt dressing	30
duck, BBQ duck and hoisin wrap	66

E

Earl Grey and ginger-steeped dates	173
eggplant and feta salad, warm	30
empanadas, tuna	17
espresso jelly	178

F

fajitas, easy beef	111
farfalle with tuna, capers and lemon cream sauce	87
fennel, tomato and fish soup with aïoli	14
figs, grilled, with honeyed mascarpone	153
fillet steak with blue cheese butter and cauliflower crush	112

fish

crisp-skin blue eye trevalla with potatoes and red coleslaw	79
farfalle with tuna, capers and lemon cream sauce	87
fennel, tomato and fish soup with aïoli	14
paprika fish with warm potato salad	128
salmon with mango–avocado salsa	108
smoked fish rarebit	74
smoked salmon and chargrilled vegetable panzanella	57
Thai fish cakes with tomato salad	13
trout in prosciutto with fennel salad	115
tuna empanadas	17
tuna Niçoise salad	65
whole fish steamed with Chinese flavours	95
five-spice lamb and sugarsnap stir-fry	135
fondue, individual	54

G

garlicky white bean brandade	45
ginger juice	22

H

haloumi, golden, with bean and olive salad	18
hazelnut and blackberry clafoutis	169
herbed lamb cutlets with steamed greens and tapénade	80

I

ice cream

passionfruit yoghurt ice cream with fruit	174
peanut brittle ice cream with chocolate sauce	149
Italian-style beef with vegetables	88

J

jelly, espresso	178

L

lamb

five-spice lamb and sugarsnap stir-fry	135
herbed lamb cutlets with steamed greens and tapénade	80
lamb, barley and mint salad	50
lamb burger with hummus and beetroot	58
lamb fillets with zucchini fritters and tahini sauce	100
lamb, lemon and rice soup	73

lamb steak with pecorino mash and artichokes	119
mini lamb roast	91
spiced lamb and yoghurt in pitta bread	10
lemon–rosemary baked custard	150

M

Malay-style chicken curry	116
minute steak with brandy cream	143

mushrooms

quick chicken and mushroom pie	92
soft cheese and walnut polenta with mushrooms	21
mussels, Thai-style steamed	38

N

noodle, beef and cashew salad	42

O

omelettes

prawn and bok choy omelette	46
soufflé omelette with ham and gruyère cheese	33
orecchiette with chicken sausage, tomato, rocket and parmesan	9

P

panzanella, smoked salmon and chargrilled vegetable	57
paprika fish with warm potato salad	128
passionfruit yoghurt ice cream with fruit	174

pasta

chargrilled squid and pasta salad	29
chicken ravioli with lemon burnt butter	144
farfalle with tuna, capers and lemon cream sauce	87
orecchiette with chicken sausage, tomato, rocket and parmesan	9
pasta with Italian sausages and balsamic glaze	103
ravioli with zucchini, sage and pine nuts	53
tortellini stracciatella	34
pastrami and fontina croque monsieur	70
peanut brittle ice cream with chocolate sauce	149
pineapple and lime millefeuille	181
piri-piri spatchcock, chargrilled	83

pear

brandy–caramel pear	158
cardamom-poached pear with ginger-biscuit cream	166

pizza

pizza dough	26
pumpkin and prosciutto pizza with hazelnut salad	26
plum and sour cream gratin	185
polenta, soft cheese and walnut, with mushrooms	21

pork

Chinese roast pork with orange sauce	99
pork, brie and apricot sandwich	37
pork sausages with cabbage caraway braise	132
roast pork with honey and pomegranate carrots	124

potatoes

crisp-skin blue eye trevalla with potatoes and red coleslaw	79
individual seafood and tarragon pies	139
lamb steak with pecorino mash and artichokes	119
paprika fish with warm potato salad	128
red flannel hash	140
veal cutlet with parsnip mash and fig salad	104
prawn and bok choy omelette	46
prune and pistachio 'sandwiches'	182
pumpkin and prosciutto pizza with hazelnut salad	26

Q

quesadillas, spiced chicken	41

R

raspberry syllabub with almond bread	165

ravioli

chicken ravioli with lemon burnt butter	144
ravioli with zucchini, sage and pine nuts	53
red flannel hash	140

S

salads

beef and cashew noodle salad	42
chargrilled squid and pasta salad	29
lamb, barley and mint salad	50
poached chicken and artichoke salad with saffron aïoli	96

roast asparagus and tofu salad with
    sesame dressing 61
sesame beef salad with avocado and
    grapefruit 22
smoked chicken Waldorf salad on bruschetta 62
smoked salmon and chargrilled vegetable
    panzanella 57
tomato salad 13
tuna Niçoise salad 65
warm eggplant and feta salad 30
salmon with mango–avocado salsa 108
sandwich, pork, brie and apricot 37
'sandwiches', prune and pistachio 182

sausages
    orecchiette with chicken sausage, tomato,
        rocket and parmesan 9
    pasta with Italian sausages and balsamic glaze 103
    pork sausages with cabbage caraway braise 132

seafood
    chargrilled squid and pasta salad 29
    individual seafood and tarragon pies 139
    prawn and bok choy omelette 46
    Thai-style steamed mussels 38
see also fish
sesame beef salad with avocado and
    grapefruit 22
smoked chicken Waldorf salad on bruschetta 62
smoked fish rarebit 74
smoked salmon and chargrilled vegetable
    panzanella 57
soufflé omelette with ham and gruyère cheese 33

soup
    chicken, corn and noodle soup 25
    fennel, tomato and fish soup with aïoli 14
    lamb, lemon and rice soup 73
    sweet potato and tofu laksa 107

spatchcock
    spatchcock with apricot couscous and zucchini 136
    chargrilled piri-piri spatchcock 83
spiced chicken quesadillas 41
spiced lamb and yoghurt in pitta bread 10
spicy capsicum and tomato bake with egg 49

stir-fries
    chilli, chicken and cashew stir-fry 120
    five-spice lamb and sugarsnap stir-fry 135
    Vietnamese lemongrass beef stir-fry 84
strawberries with ricotta cream and mint 154
sweet potato and tofu laksa 107
syllabub, raspberry, with almond bread 165

T
Thai fish cakes with tomato salad 13
Thai-style steamed mussels 38
tofu
    caramel tofu with peanuts and ginger 69
    roast asparagus and tofu salad with
        sesame dressing 61
    sweet potato and tofu laksa 107
torrijas with honey cream 177
tortellini stracciatella 34
trifle, cherry-brioche 170
trout in prosciutto with fennel salad 115
tuna empanadas 17
tuna Niçoise salad 65

V
veal cutlet with parsnip mash and fig salad 104
Vietnamese lemongrass beef stir-fry 84

Y
yoghurt
    passionfruit yoghurt ice cream with fruit 174
    spiced lamb and yoghurt in pitta bread 10
    yoghurt chicken with Indian spices 127

The **My Kitchen** series is packed with sensational flavours, simple methods and vibrant photographs. What's more, these easy, inexpensive and well-tested recipes use only commonly available ingredients and fresh seasonal produce. And because cooking should be a joy, there's a little bit of magic in these recipes too, in the form of smart short cuts and clever substitutions.

Single Serves contains fabulous meals, made for just one person. There are great ideas for snacks and light meals, as well as mini roasts and baked dinners, and impressive desserts. Just occasionally there is an extra serve included, so lunch is already made for the next day or dinner's in the freezer for later in the week.

ISBN 978-1741964448

9 781741 964448

MURDOCH BOOKS